NATIONAL
ACADEMIES

Sciences
Engineering
Medicine

NATIONAL
ACADEMIES
PRESS
Washington, DC

Developing an Agenda for Population Aging and Social Research in Low- and Middle-Income Countries (LMICs)

Erin Hammers Forstag, *Rapporteur*

Committee on Population

Division of Behavioral and Social Sciences and Education

Proceedings of a Workshop

NATIONAL ACADEMIES PRESS 500 Fifth Street, NW Washington, DC 20001

This activity was supported by a contract between the National Academy of Sciences and the National Institute on Aging (HHSN263201800029I/ 75N98022F00009). Any opinions, findings, conclusions, or recommendations expressed in this publication do not necessarily reflect the views of any organization or agency that provided support for the project.

International Standard Book Number-13: 978-0-309-71343-6
International Standard Book Number-10: 0-309-71343-9
Digital Object Identifier: https://doi.org/10.17226/27415

This publication is available from the National Academies Press, 500 Fifth Street, NW, Keck 360, Washington, DC 20001; (800) 624-6242 or (202) 334-3313; http://www.nap.edu.

Suggested citation: National Academies of Sciences, Engineering, and Medicine. 2024. *Developing an Agenda for Population Aging and Social Research in Low- and Middle-Income Countries (LMICs): Proceedings of a Workshop*. Washington, DC: The National Academies Press. https://doi. org/10.17226/27415.

The **National Academy of Sciences** was established in 1863 by an Act of Congress, signed by President Lincoln, as a private, nongovernmental institution to advise the nation on issues related to science and technology. Members are elected by their peers for outstanding contributions to research. Dr. Marcia McNutt is president.

The **National Academy of Engineering** was established in 1964 under the charter of the National Academy of Sciences to bring the practices of engineering to advising the nation. Members are elected by their peers for extraordinary contributions to engineering. Dr. John L. Anderson is president.

The **National Academy of Medicine** (formerly the Institute of Medicine) was established in 1970 under the charter of the National Academy of Sciences to advise the nation on medical and health issues. Members are elected by their peers for distinguished contributions to medicine and health. Dr. Victor J. Dzau is president.

The three Academies work together as the **National Academies of Sciences, Engineering, and Medicine** to provide independent, objective analysis and advice to the nation and conduct other activities to solve complex problems and inform public policy decisions. The National Academies also encourage education and research, recognize outstanding contributions to knowledge, and increase public understanding in matters of science, engineering, and medicine.

Learn more about the National Academies of Sciences, Engineering, and Medicine at **www.nationalacademies.org**.

COMMITTEE ON POPULATION

Reviewers

This Proceedings of a Workshop was reviewed in draft form by individuals chosen for their diverse perspectives and technical expertise. The purpose of this independent review is to provide candid and critical comments that will assist the National Academies of Sciences, Engineering, and Medicine in making each published proceedings as sound as possible and to ensure that it meets the institutional standards for quality, objectivity, evidence, and responsiveness to the charge. The review comments and draft manuscript remain confidential to protect the integrity of the process.

We thank the following individual for their review of this proceedings:

REBECA WONG, University of Texas Medical Branch at Galveston

Although the reviewer listed above provided many constructive comments and suggestions, she was not asked to endorse the content of the proceedings nor did she see the final draft before its release. We also thank staff member **LIDA BENINSON** for reviewing and providing helpful comments on this manuscript.

The review of this proceedings was overseen by **JUDITH SELTZER,** University of California, Los Angeles. She was responsible for making certain that an independent examination of this proceedings was carried out in accordance with standards of the National Academies and that all review comments were carefully considered. Responsibility for the final content rests entirely with the rapporteur and the National Academies.

Acknowledgments

Funding for the workshop was provided by the Division of Behavioral and Social Research of the National Institute on Aging (NIA), and NIA staff provided substantial input to the workshop. The planning committee thanks Minki Chatterji and Charlie Le at NIA for being generous with their time and attention in answering the committee's questions and providing vital information to develop the scope and content of the workshop.

The planning committee is grateful to all the speakers for sharing their experiences and knowledge by providing high-quality and relevant presentations for this workshop. A video playlist of the workshop as well as links to all presentations can be found at https://www.nationalacademies.org/event/09-07-2023/developing-an-agenda-for-population-aging-and-social-research-in-low-and-middle-income-countries-lmics-a-workshop. Finally, the workshop and proceedings would not be possible without help from knowledgeable and talented National Academies staff who provided guidance, shared best practices, and assisted in navigating institutional processes and procedures.

This proceedings was prepared by the workshop rapporteur as a factual summary of what occurred at the workshop. The planning committee's role was limited to planning and convening the workshop. The views contained in the proceedings are those of individual participants and do not necessarily represent the views of all workshop participants, the planning committee, NIA, or the National Academies.

Contents

Box and Figures

Acronyms and Abbreviations

AD/ADRD	Alzheimer's disease and related dementias
BA	biological age
BSR	Division of Behavioral and Social Research (National Institute of Aging)
CA	chronological age
CHARLS	China Health and Retirement Longitudinal Study
CPOP	Committee on Population
DATASUS	health data from the National Health System
DFLE	disability-free life expectancy
DPPIA	Data Protection & Privacy Impact Assessment
ELSA	English Longitudinal Study of Ageing
ELSI[1]	Brazilian Longitudinal Study of Aging
ENSANUT[2]	Mexican National Survey of Health and Nutrition
GDP	gross domestic product

---

[1] ELSI is a Portuguese acronym, however, for accessibility and consistency the common English definition is provided here and used throughout the report.

[2] ENSANUT is a Spanish acronym, however, for accessibility and consistency the common English definition is provided here and used throughout the report.

HAALSI	Health and Aging in Africa: A Longitudinal Study in South Africa
HDSS	health and demographic surveillance system
HMIS	Health Management Information System
HRS	Health and Retirement Study
IDB	Inter-American Development Bank
INSPIRE Network	Implementation Network for Sharing Population Information from Research Entities
LMICs	low- and middle-income countries
LOSHAK	Longitudinal Study of Health and Aging in Kenya
LSMS	Living Standards Measurement Study
LSMS-ISA	Living Standards Measurement Study—Integrated Surveys on Agriculture
MHAS	Mexican Health and Aging Study
NIA	National Institute on Aging
PAHO	Pan American Health Organization
PM-JAY	Pradhan Mantri Jan Arogya Yojana
RSBY	Rashtriya Swasthya Bima Yojana
SES	socioeconomic status
SHARE	Survey of Health, Ageing and Retirement in Europe
STAR	Study of the Tsunami Aftermath and Recovery
WHO	World Health Organization

1

Introduction

In September 2023, the Committee on Population (CPOP) at the National Academies of Sciences, Engineering, and Medicine held a workshop, *Developing an Agenda for Population Aging and Social Research in Low- and Middle-Income Countries (LMICs)*. The idea for the workshop grew out of conversations between CPOP and the National Institute on Aging (NIA), which led to the statement of task for the activity: see Box 1-1. The goal was to assemble a group of experts to discuss the research agenda on aging, with an emphasis on LMICs. The explicit goal of the workshop was to identify the most promising directions for behavioral and social research and data infrastructure investments for studying life-course health, aging, and Alzheimer's disease and Alzheimer's disease and related dementias (AD/ADRD) in LMICs.

The workshop was arranged around three broad themes: inequality, family change, and climate change. The workshop agenda is in Appendix A; biographical sketches of the interdisciplinary planning committee that convened to organize the workshop are in Appendix B.

BACKGROUND

The planning committee chair, Rebeca Wong (University of Texas Medical Branch), opened the first session by describing the interactive process with the National Academies and NIA that led to the workshop. The workshop goal was to identify priorities for future research and data collection in order to strengthen the evidence base for policy making.

Box 1-1
Statement of Task

A planning committee of the National Academies of Sciences, Engineering, and Medicine will organize and execute a two-day public workshop that will bring together an interdisciplinary group of experts to discuss behavioral and social research and data priorities for studying life-course health, aging, and Alzheimer's Disease and related dementias in low- and middle-income countries (LMICs). The workshop will focus on three priority topics: inequality, environmental exposures, and changes in family structure. The workshop will:

- Identify research priorities related to the impacts of inequality, environmental exposure, and family changes on the health and well-being of older populations in LMICs, with an emphasis on how existing data resources may be leveraged to address these topics.
- Discuss how country-specific research in LMICs can create a better understanding of how different social environments and public policies influence health outcomes related to aging; and how findings from country-specific LMIC research may be generalized to other settings, including the United States.
- Identify new conceptual, theoretical, methodological, and/or data investments that are needed to move from purely descriptive cross-national analyses to more causal analyses that create a better understanding of how inequality, environmental exposures, and changing family structures impact health and well-being at older ages in LMICs.
- Identify data (early-life prospective data or retrospective data from current older cohorts) that may be of interest for examining life-course trajectories of development and aging in LMICs.

After the workshop, a proceedings of the workshop, summarizing the presentations and discussions at the workshop, will be prepared by a designated rapporteur in accordance with institutional guidelines.

Amy Kelley (NIA) shared the perspective of NIA, noting that the agency is the part of the National Institutes of Health that leads the federal government in conducting and supporting research on the health and well-being of older people. Among other topics, she said, NIA funds research to study aging in different social, cultural, and economic contexts in order to support the identification of behavioral, social risk, and protective factors that are associated with aging and life-course outcomes, including those related to AD/ARD. There has been less research in LMICs than in high-income countries, thus the workshop's focus on LMICs. One challenge for research in this area, said Kelley, is that there is limited availability of representative longitudinal data; one goal of the workshop is to identify and discuss potential research opportunities that would be possible with more representative longitudinal data. Funding this research, she said, will improve the health of older people in the United States and worldwide.

Kelley described some of the efforts in which NIA has invested in research in LMICs, including:

- the Health and Retirement Study (HRS) International Family of Studies: harmonized, cross-national research on the drivers of aging and dementia;
- the Gateway to Global Aging Data: free public resource designed to facilitate cross-national and longitudinal studies on aging; and
- the Harmonized Cognitive Assessment Protocol Network: international research collaboration aimed at measuring and understanding dementia risks within longitudinal studies of aging.

These types of studies can help systematically examine the social and economic determinants of health, and how these determinants can produce disparities in the trajectory of aging, health, and survival, said Kelley. In addition, there are a number of social science questions that can be uniquely addressed with cross-national comparative studies, as well as country-specific studies in LMICs. Kelley expressed her hope that this workshop would help to guide the research agenda in these areas for the coming years.

Lis Nielsen (NIA) followed up on her colleague's remarks by highlighting a few additional areas of interest at the Division of Behavioral and Social Research (BSR) at NIA. In the last several years, said Nielsen, BSR has accelerated its efforts to develop research resources and tools in order to enable the rigorous study of how macro-level social factors shape the process of aging, both in the United States and globally. These BSR efforts were stimulated in part by recommendations from a committee of experts convened by the National Advisory Council on Aging, she said. The committee urged BSR to intensify research focused on the effects on aging of major social shifts, including:[1]

- changing family lives of older adults,
- the rising number of older adults living alone,
- the rapidly changing nature of work,
- growing income inequality,
- trends in ageism and discrimination,
- immigration,
- climate change, and

---

[1]The committee's report can be found at https://www.nia.nih.gov/sites/default/files/2020-02/2019-BSR-Review-Committee-Report-508.pdf

- the macro-social sources of worsening mental and physical health and mortality.

After this report's release, Nielsen said, the COVID-19 pandemic and other global disruptions highlighted the fragility and the resilience of older populations around the globe, the interconnectedness of different societies, and the need to strengthen the collective search for innovative ways to meet the challenges and opportunities of global aging. She highlighted two recent publications that are the result of NIA's partnership with CPOP: a consensus study on rising midlife mortality rates in the United States (National Academies, 2021) and a workshop summary on developing a research agenda on structural racism (National Academies, 2022). Nielsen said that she hoped that this workshop would help NIA formulate strategies for staying at the cutting edge of this work and building on the existing investments to develop high-value data infrastructure to meet the needs of the broader international aging research community.

Another NIA representative, Minki Chatterji, expanded on some of the projects that Nielsen and Kelley had mentioned. BSR, said Chatterji, engages the research community in order to help identify program priorities. For example, BSR is working toward achieving the implementation milestones for AD/ADRD that were recommended by the research community. BSR's emphasis on global aging research addresses these types of community-identified priorities by examining how behavioral and social factors influence outcomes in varying social, cultural, and economic contexts. Chatterji explained that global and cross-national research can give clues about which policies or contexts lead to better outcomes, which can help people both in the United States and across the globe.

The HRS International Family of Studies are a major piece of this global research, said Chatterji.[2] These studies use nationally representative samples and follow participants over time with a multidisciplinary focus. While the studies are not identical across countries, they are harmonized in order to be comparable. The data from this research are publicly available, she said. While these studies have been conducted in over 40 countries, they have not yet included many LMICs. It is important to study LMICs, Chatterji explained, because some aspects of the social, cultural, and economic contexts are very different in LMICs than in the United States, and these differences can help illuminate what factors lead to different outcomes. For example, the differences between older adults in sub-Saharan Africa and those in the United States, which might lead to different outcomes, include more rural living, more time in multigenerational households and caring for younger people, staying in the labor force longer, living in countries with

---

[2]https://www.nia.nih.gov/research/dbsr/global-aging/hrs-international-family-studies-and-harmonized-cognitive-assessment-protocol

weak health systems and challenges accessing health care, and lower levels of life satisfaction and higher levels of depression.

Chatterji said that the NIA hopes to hear from experts at the workshop about what types of research the NIA should prioritize, particularly in the areas identified for focus: inequality, environmental exposures, and family change. In addition to future directions for research, Chatterji pointed out that there may be a need for investments in infrastructure in order to facilitate research in all areas.

SETTING THE STAGE

To lay a foundation for the rest of the workshop, the keynote presentation by Lisa Berkman (Harvard University) introduced the issues and identified areas of critical importance. She began by emphasizing the importance of focusing on successful aging societies. A successful society is one that facilitates and develops the capacity of people to age successfully. Research that looks at aging in a decontextualized way focuses only on the few individuals who have the resources to age successfully and leaves out the rest. She explained that a successful aging society is "not just about old people"; rather, it functions effectively on a societal level for people of all ages. Berkman shared a quote from work by the MacArthur Foundation Research Network on an Aging Society (Rowe, 2015, p. 5):

As America ages, policy-makers' preoccupations with the future costs of Medicare and Socia Security grow. But neglected by this focus are critically important and broader societal issues such as intergenerational relations within society and the family, rising inequality and lack of opportunity, productivity in late life (work or volunteering), and human capital development (lifelong education and skills training). Equally important, there is almost no acknowledgment of the substantial benefits and potential of an aging society.

Based on this work, Berkman identified five hallmarks of a successful aging society:

- functions effectively at a societal level;
- addresses issues of transition to cohesive, productive, secure, and equitable aging society;
- requires adaptation of core societal institutions (e.g., education);
- identifies and builds on positive contributions of an aging society; and
- adopts a life-course perspective by looking at people across the age spectrum, as well as at intergenerational issues.

Berkman noted that research on successful aging societies requires the collection of contextual-level variables that are often readily available; it does not necessarily require asking more of an "already-burdened set of participants." In choosing countries for focused research, Berkman said that some countries are ripe for studying aging right now, while others should be prioritized for investments in future research. For example, she said, between 2025 and 2050, Mexico will undergo the transition from a younger population to an older one: see Figure 1-1. In prioritizing countries for research on the transition to an aging society, Berkman said that the focus should be on countries that are "on the runway" by 2050.

There are numerous social and physical determinants of health that can be studied in relation to aging, said Berkman. She shared data and findings from selected studies on several of these determinants. The first study she discussed looked at the effects of the amount of education on child health and adult mortality (Pradhan et al., 2017). It found that education of females had an "enormous" impact on mortality, particularly in low-income countries: see Figure 1-2. Specifically, the study showed that "14 percent of reductions in overall under-five mortality, 30 percent of reductions in adult female mortality, and 31 percent of reductions in adult male mortality can be attributed to gains in female schooling" (Pradhan et al., 2017, p. 427).

Another study used data from the Health and Aging in Africa: A Longitudinal Study in South Africa to look at the impact of multiple determinants—including education, employment, marital status, and health behaviors—on cognitive impairment (Kobayashi et al., 2021). This study found that education is "incredibly important," as is literacy: see Figure 1-3, which shows those with education had the lowest relative incidence of cognitive impairment. These findings show the "lifelong impact of investing in education," said Berkman.

Data from the Mexican Health and Aging Study have been used to look at how lifetime socioeconomic status (SES) affects trajectories of functional limitations and depressive symptoms in middle age: see Figures 1-4 and 1-5. Berkman said that these findings show that the effects of SES are "quite complicated," and it can be challenging to tease out the separate effects of education, wealth, employment, and other factors.

Another important factor that has been studied as a determinant of health is adverse childhood experiences, said Berkman. A study from China found that each adverse experience contributes to an increasing risk of multimorbidity—the co-occurrence of two or more chronic conditions—(Lin et al., 2021): see Figure 1-6. She noted that there is a need to acknowledge the "huge number" of adverse events that people have experienced in many countries, including war, apartheid, famine, poverty, and disruption of family life and connections.

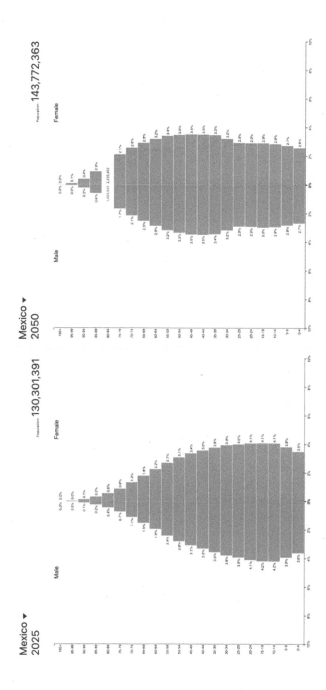

FIGURE 1-1 Mexico population pyramid, 2025 and 2050.
SOURCE: ©2023 by PopulationPyramid.net. Reprinted under Creative Commons license CC BY 3.0 IGO: http://creativecommons.org/licenses/by/3.0/igo/. Left panel: https://www.populationpyramid.net/mexico/2025/, right panel: https://www.populationpyramid.net/mexico/2050/

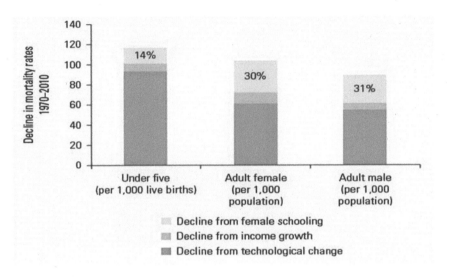

FIGURE 1-2 Decline in mortality attributable to increases in female schooling in 92 countries, 1970–2010.
NOTE: Data are from 92 low- and middle-income countries, each of which included observations at 5-year intervals between 1970 and 2010. For full list, see https://dcp-3.org/sites/default/files/chapters/Annex%2030A.%20Countries%20in%20Regression%20Analysis.pdf
SOURCE: Pradhan et al. (2017, Figure 30.1). Reprinted under Creative Commons Attribution 3.0 IGO license (CC BY 3.0 IGO) http://creativecommons.org/licenses/by/3.0/igo

Berkman said that one of the most promising areas for future research is using natural experiments[3] to look at the impact of policy on health outcomes. For example, a study in South Africa found that men who were newly eligible for pensions—due to lowering of the eligibility age—had higher than expected cognitive function (Jock et al., 2023). The study suggested cash transfers may hold promise as potential interventions to promote healthy cognitive aging.[4] These types of policy "experiments" are a very powerful tool for learning more about the effects of interventions on health. In addition, she said, this type of research does not rely on people's memory, which can be unreliable.

Another type of research that does not require asking people about their individual exposure is research on environmental conditions. For example, a study in China showed decreases in cognitive function with exposure to ambient particulate matter for middle-age and elderly Chinese

---

[3]For details, see Craig et al. (2017).
[4]The change in pension eligibility allowed a comparison of men who received pensions at a younger age than prior cohorts under the assumption that the policy change was exogenous, that is analogous to an experimental treatment.

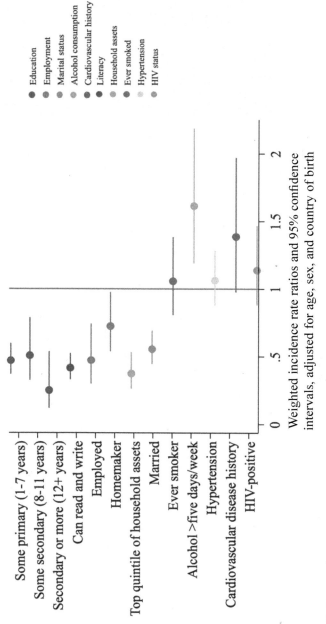

FIGURE 1-3 Relative cognitive impairment incidence by social, economic, and health-related factors in South Africa.
SOURCE: Adapted from Kobayashi et al. (2021, Table 1).

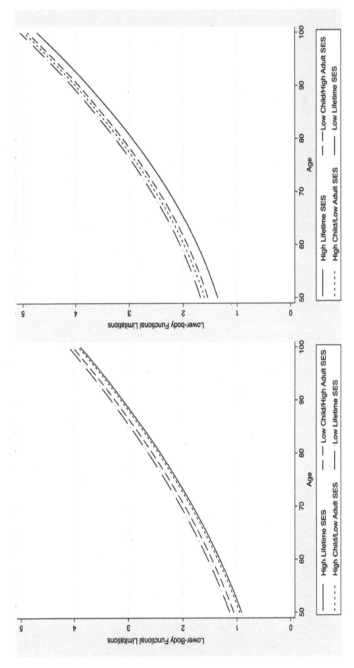

FIGURE 1-4 Functional limitations over age by lifetime socioeconomic status (SES) for men (left panel) and women (right panel) in Mexico.
SOURCE: Torres et al. (2018, Figures 1C and 1D). Reprinted with permission.

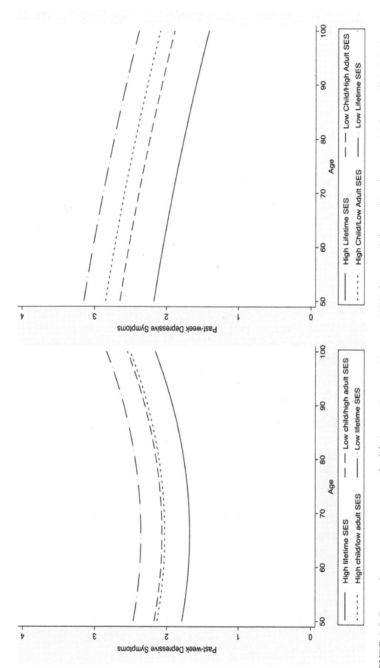

FIGURE 1-5 Depressive symptoms over age by lifetime socioeconomic status (SES) for men (left panel) and women (right panel) in Mexico.
SOURCE: Torres et al. (2018, Figures 1A and 1B). Reprinted with permission.

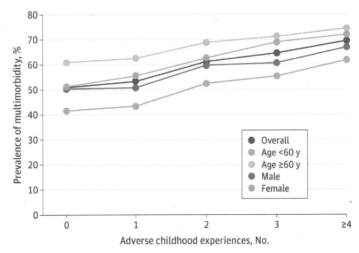

FIGURE 1-6 Adverse childhood experiences and subsequent chronic diseases in China.
SOURCE: Lin et al. (2021, Figure 2). Reprinted with permission.

adults (Yao et al., 2022). It is essential, said Berkman, that researchers study the impact of the environment on aging health; climate change has huge consequences for people in LMICs, and it is critical to understand how policies could help or hurt these populations. She also noted that researchers looking at social determinants sometimes ignore the important role of health systems. A study in sub-Saharan African looked at how easier access to antihypertensive treatment could improve blood pressure control (Parati et al., 2023). It is essential, said Berkman, that researchers consider the role of multiple stakeholders—including governments, health care systems, the scientific community, development partners, communities, and individuals—when studying the factors that affect healthy aging.

In conclusion, Berkman encouraged researchers to identify demographic transitions in societies and to focus on major institutions that influence change, including educational, economic, political, environmental, and health systems. She emphasized the importance of using the perspective of an aging society rather than focusing on individual factors. However, she noted that societies are heterogeneous, and it is important to look both at averages as well as differences within populations. The distributional differences can sometimes "tell a more interesting story," she said, and can expand knowledge about healthy aging for both individuals and populations as a whole.

2

The Role of Inequality

Key Points Highlighted by the Presenters

- The patterns of health inequalities in low- and middle-income countries (LMICs), such as Brazil and Mexico, are changing rapidly across birth cohorts; the social determinants of health inequalities in this context are complex and need to be considered with an intersectionality approach leveraging longitudinal data. **(AVILA)**

- Gradients in health change over time and may be exacerbated by shocks, such as natural disasters or pandemics. More research is needed on how health policies can shed light on what causes changes in gradients. **(SUDHARSANAN)**

- There is a need for more micro-level causal research of policy effects on long-run health and inequality in LMICs, and this should be complemented with expanded macro-level research that aggregates health and inequality effects across policies. **(DOW)**

The first session of the workshop focused on how inequality—in income, wealth, access to opportunities or resources—affects the health and well-being of older populations in low- and middle-income countries (LMICs). Speakers and participants had been given a set of questions to guide their presentations and discussion:

- How does income inequality affect the health and well-being of older populations in LMICs in the context of changing and evolving economies?
- How are changes in the nature of work influencing disability, dementia, and mortality?
- Are there trends, and are they actionable?

INEQUALITIES AMONG OLDER ADULTS IN LATIN AMERICA

In Latin America, older adults experience the burden of infectious and chronic diseases, and the pension, health care, and education systems are not prepared for the changes of an aging society, said Jaqueline Avila (University of Massachusetts Boston). She made the case for studying Brazil and Mexico as a way of understanding the larger region; Mexico and Brazil make up half the population in Latin America, they are the largest economies in the region, and they have large social inequalities. While populations are aging all over the world, the phenomenon is particularly strong in Brazil and Mexico. Compared with the United States, the older populations of Brazil and Mexico are growing faster than the younger populations: see Figure 2-1. This rapid change poses significant challenges, said Avila, especially for the social protection benefits that rely on the contribution of younger individuals. Further, Mexico and Brazil are aging fast in a low-income context; they have much lower gross national income per capita than many other countries. However, by 2050, the share of the population 65 years and older in Brazil and Mexico will be similar, if not greater, than the older adult population in higher-income countries: see Figure 2-2.

There are a number of sources for data to study population aging and health in Mexico and Brazil, said Avila. For Brazil, these sources include the Longitudinal Study of Aging (ELSI), the National Health Survey (PNS), the National Household Sample Survey (PNAD), health data from the national health system (DATASUS), and regional or city-level data. In Mexico, data sources include the Mexican Health and Aging Study (MHAS), the National Survey of Health and Nutrition (ENSANUT), and regional and city-level data.[1]

Evidence from these datasets shows that older adults in Brazil and Mexico have similar characteristics, said Avila, with comparable rates of chronic disease and similarly low levels of education. In addition, there are common social determinants of health inequalities in both countries, including education, income/wealth, gender, health insurance, and within-country

---

[1]For more information on surveys, see: ELSI (https://elsi.cpqrr.fiocruz.br/en/home-english/), PNAD (https://www.ibge.gov.br/en/statistics/social/labor/20620-summary-of-indicators-pnad2.html), DATASUS (https://datasus.saude.gov.br/), MHAS (https://www.mhasweb.org/Home/index.aspx), and ENSANUT (https://en.www.inegi.org.mx/programas/ensanut/2018/).

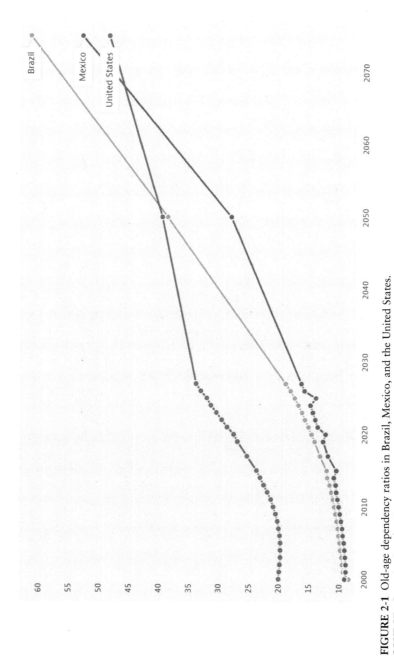

FIGURE 2-1 Old-age dependency ratios in Brazil, Mexico, and the United States.

SOURCE: Organisation for Economic Co-operation and Development (2023), Old-age dependency ratio (indicator). https://doi.org/10.1787/e0255c98-en (Accessed on 1 September 2023).

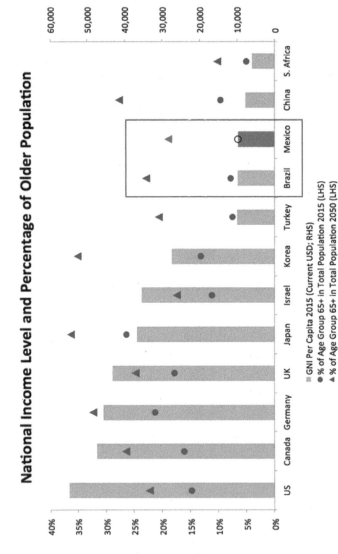

FIGURE 2-2 National income level and percentage of older populations in select countries.
NOTE: RHS, label for right y axis; LHS, label for left y axis.
SOURCE: AARP International (no date, p. 2). Reprinted with permission.

regional differences. Avila detailed how these social determinants affect health inequalities across common risk factors (e.g., tobacco, obesity) and chronic diseases (e.g., diabetes, Alzheimer's disease and related dementias) in Brazil and Mexico.

Education is the most studied disparity in Mexico and Brazil; both countries have a high proportion of older adults with zero years of education, and functional illiteracy is prevalent even among people with a few years of education. There are also complex interactions between education and gender on health risk factors, said Avila. For example, for men 50 years and older in both countries, the prevalence of obesity increases as education increases. For women, the prevalence of obesity increases along with education in Mexico but decreases as education increases in Brazil. There are large gender disparities in smoking in both countries, with men much more likely to smoke than women. However, the gender gap is closing at every education level in Brazil; and, in Mexico, women with more education are more likely to smoke compared to Brazil.

One clear impact of education for both men and women is in the area of cognitive impairment. Individuals with at least 1 year of education have far lower levels of cognitive impairment than individuals with 0 years of education: see Figure 2-3. However, the benefit of higher education for men in Brazil is lower than the benefit for men in Mexico. The complexity of these data, said Avila, demonstrates the importance of looking at the intersection of multiple characteristics when studying social determinants of health in Latin America.

Income and wealth are also social determinants of large health inequalities in both Brazil and Mexico. Social protection programs, including social security, play an important role in reducing social inequalities for older adults, said Avila. In Brazil, social security is comprehensive and universal; it covers more than 80% of older adults and is the main source of income for them. As a result, there are low levels of poverty among older adults in Brazil. However, she noted that there are challenges ahead due to the increasing old-age dependency ratio: an increasing number of beneficiaries will be relying on a decreasing number of workers. In Mexico, social security is fragmented and tied to one's employer. People in the large informal work sector do not have access to social security and must rely on supplemental income programs. There are high levels of poverty among older adults in Mexico. Avila said that the different approaches between these countries may give insight on how to best address income and wealth inequalities.

Health insurance systems are another factor that can help narrow health disparities, said Avila. There are major challenges ahead for both Mexico and Brazil, with individuals living longer with a higher prevalence of chronic disease. As with social protection programs, the differences in approaches between Mexico and Brazil may provide insights about the impact

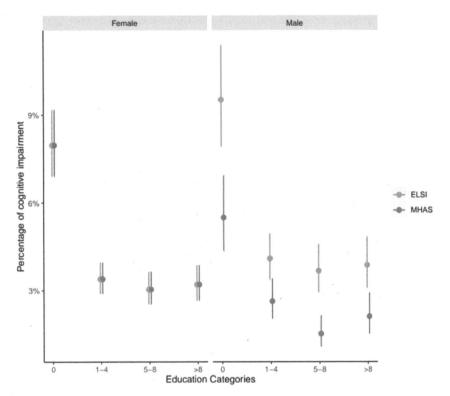

FIGURE 2-3 Association between education categories and cognitive impairment by sex and cohort in Brazil and Mexico.
NOTE: ELSI = Longitudinal Study of Aging; MHAS = Mexican Health and Aging Study.
SOURCE: Adapted from Gonçalves et al. (2023, Figures 1 and 2). Reprinted with permission.

of different policy choices. Brazil has universal health insurance, although there are regional differences in good access to care. People with private insurance are wealthier and are more likely to visit specialists than those who rely on public insurance and receive basic primary care. In Mexico, health insurance is fragmented and tied to one's employer. Before health care reform in 2003, there was a large uninsured population. There have been significant improvements in primary care use and diagnostics, but limited improvements in chronic disease treatment. In both countries, said Avila, the question remains whether the health insurance system is prepared to deal with an aging population with chronic diseases.

When discussing inequality within countries, it is critical to acknowledge that there are important geographical differences and disparities. In Brazil, regional differences are a major source of inequality. Macro-regions are experiencing the pace of the demographic and epidemiologic transition to an aging population differently, and the North and Northeast areas have poorer access to health care and greater mortality than the South, Midwest, and Southeast regions. In Mexico, differences between urban and rural areas are a major source of inequality. People in rural areas have poorer access to health care, lower education, more poverty, and poorer health than people in urban areas, while people in urban areas have higher rates of obesity and tobacco and alcohol use than those in rural areas.

Across all social determinants, Avila emphasized the importance of studying trends and identifying cohort differences. Studying younger cohorts helps to understand the aging scenario in the coming decades. Social determinants of health inequalities across cohorts are changing fast, and demographic and epidemiologic changes in new cohorts will affect chronic disease burden. For example, obesity prevalence is increasing for men and women in Mexico, and middle-aged adults have higher obesity prevalence than older adults. In Brazil, men with higher education have been quitting smoking, but educated women lag behind in this trend.

Avila closed by identifying several areas to prioritize for research on aging in Latin America, focusing on actionable items with data that are already available:

- leveraging cohort comparisons with cross-sectional and longitudinal data;
- considering multiple social determinants and their interactions;
- using the evidence to promote interventions to decrease regional differences;
- developing methods to validate self-reported conditions; and
- promoting the use of linked longitudinal data with administrative records.

SOCIOECONOMIC STATUS GRADIENTS IN INDIA

Gradients in health are dynamic and change over time, said Nikkil Sudharsanan (Technical University of Munich). However, much of the literature on gradients in LMICs is based on snapshots in time. This gap is due to a lack of available data, but it gives the impression that gradients are static. To illustrate the dynamic nature of gradients in health, Sudharsanan presented data on obesity and associated outcomes in India at different points of time.

A decades-old idea, called the "reverse hypothesis," posits that cardiovascular risk factors such as obesity are concentrated in the advantaged segments of the population in lower-income countries. As a country develops, the concentration flattens out and eventually flips so that risk factors are more prevalent in the less advantaged segments of society. The limitation of most research that has tested this hypothesis, said Sudharsanan, is that the research compares countries or regions that are at different levels of development, rather than looking at a single country at different points of time. This kind of comparison relies on a potentially faulty assumption that countries at different levels of development represent what a single country would experience as it develops.

Obesity, Diabetes, Hypertension, and Smoking

To address this limitation, Sudharsanan and his colleagues looked at gradients in risk factors in India by analyzing data from 2015, 2019, and 2021. They used the National Family and Health Surveys and looked at four outcomes: obesity, diabetes, hypertension, and smoking. The dataset contains over 1.5 million observations, with about 800,000 people per wave.

Sudharsanan said the data on obesity demonstrate a "striking pattern." Being overweight is much more common among wealthier populations, higher-education groups, and people who live in urban areas. However, the gradients are "flattening in a very short amount of time," he said. Over a 6-year period, obesity has grown much more in the disadvantaged populations than in the advantaged populations. For example, obesity grew about 8% in urban areas but 30% in rural areas.

The pattern with diabetes is similar, said Sudharsanan. Over the course of the study, prevalence was still higher among the richer populations, but it is shifting over time: the poorest households experienced a 24% *increase* in diabetes while the richest households experienced a 7% *decrease*. Sudharsanan noted that patterns can sometimes look different depending on what measure of socioeconomic status (SES) is used (e.g., education, wealth, income).

The reverse hypothesis is most clearly demonstrated with rates of hypertension. The richer populations have higher hypertension, but over the 6-year period covered by the study, richer populations have seen a decrease while poorer populations have experienced an increase. The gradient is "rapidly flipping."

Smoking is the one risk factor that is more prevalent among the disadvantaged segments of the population, though it is decreasing across all segments. However, similar to the other gradients, smoking has decreased at a much faster rate among more advantaged segments of the population than among less advantaged segments of the population. In this area, the gradient has already flipped and is getting worse over time.

This research, said Sudharsanan, has presented strong evidence in favor of the reverse hypothesis. Over just a 6-year period, rapid changes have occurred in the prevalence of multiple health risk factors, and the trends are clear. These findings suggest three new questions for future research, he said: (1) Are there contexts where gradients have stabilized, or are gradients always in flux? (2) Given the likelihood that gradients are changing rapidly, how should one look at studies that use cross-sectional snapshots in time to look at inequalities? (3) How do gradients of cardiovascular risk factors interact with health care to produce mortality gradients? Sudharsanan explained that while rates of risk factors are higher among the more advantaged segments of the population, their mortality is not higher; this suggests that access to health care and treatment is moderating the impact of risk factors.

The Effect of Shocks

Based on the idea that gradients can change over time, Sudharsanan and his colleagues set out to understand how shocks can expand gradients. Using National Family Health Survey data from India, they looked at under-5 mortality and over-5 mortality to generate life expectancy estimates by social group and caste. These data were collected both before and after the COVID-19 pandemic began. This inadvertent timing, he explained, allowed researchers to look at pre- and post-COVID mortality, and compare changes among groups.

Sudharsanan and his colleagues found that all groups lost life expectancy after COVID-19, but the loss was far greater among the disadvantaged populations. Between 2019 and 2020, the scheduled castes, scheduled tribes, and Muslims lost around 4 years, while higher caste groups lost only 1 to 1.5 years: see Figure 2-4. An already "pretty striking" mortality disadvantage grew even larger because of the shock of the COVID-19 pandemic, he said. This phenomenon is not unique to India; it was also seen in the United States in expanded mortality gradients by race and ethnicity. It is also not unique to pandemics, he said; disasters such as climate-induced heat or weather patterns often disproportionately affect those who are already disadvantaged.

These findings suggest several intriguing questions for future research, said Sudharsanan. First, are these expansions of gradients inevitable, or are there ways to buffer against expansions? Second, will gradients return to their previous levels, or does the expansion linger or worsen over time?

Policy Challenges to Addressing Inequalities

It is clear there are large inequalities in India, said Sudharsanan. India has worked to address these inequalities through policy and is a "frontrunner" in the area of large social health insurance programs. Around 2007,

22

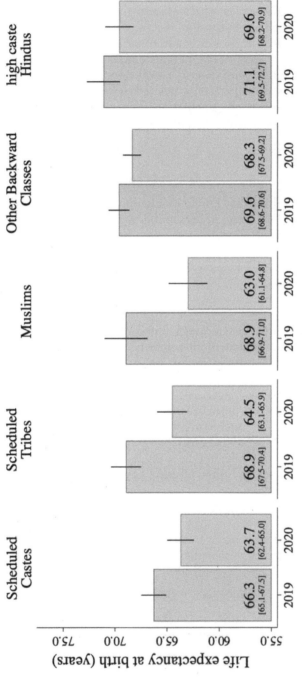

FIGURE 2-4 Life expectancy by social group in India, 2019–2020.
SOURCE: Gupta et al. (2023, Figure 4a). Reprinted with permission.

India implemented Rashtriya Swasthya Bima Yojana (RSBY), which evolved into Pradhan Mantri Jan Arogya Yojana (PM-JAY). Both are government-funded health insurance programs with explicit pro-poor eligibility criteria. The programs seek to overenroll poorer households with the aim of addressing health inequalities. However, these programs have faced major challenges in both targeting and uptake, he said. First, it can be difficult to reliably identify poor households for enrollment. Second, the most disadvantaged groups tend to underenroll, despite their higher need. Working with the Tamil Nadu state government to figure out why tribal populations and urban slum residents are significantly underenrolled in the government insurance program, his colleagues found that it is likely due to "hassle costs": that is, it is difficult for these groups to find the enrollment sites, travel to the site, and figure out how to enroll.

A recent paper on noncontributory social health insurance coverage in India found that the group that the policy explicitly targets—the poorest quintile—has lower enrollment than other groups (Mohanty et al., 2023). With the transition from the RSBY to the PM-JAY, enrollment increased among all groups: see Figure 2-5. However, the gradient remained, particularly across wealth. When considering policy solutions to inequality, it can be challenging to find a solution that minimizes gradients.

Even if universal health coverage was in place and people from all segments of the population had insurance, there are still gradients when it comes to accessing high-quality health care, said Sudharsanan. A study by Das and Mohpal (2016), looking at how far households had to travel to reach care and how competent these accessible providers were, found that high-SES households can reach a medium-skill provider at a much shorter distance than a low-SES household: see Figure 2-6. Even more striking, he said, is that if high-SES households travel farther, they can reach the most competent providers, whereas low-SES households cannot access these providers even when traveling longer distances. There are challenges in targeting and enrolling low-SES households, and even those who are enrolled face disparities in access to high-quality care.

In conclusion, Sudharsanan offered his thoughts on what is needed to address inequalities. First, he said, we need "non-hand-wavy explanations" for levels and changes in gradients. He explained that researchers spend a great deal of time figuring out how to precisely measure gradients, but then "hand wave our way through why those gradients exist, why they are changing over time, and what we can do about them." Second, there is a need to closely examine the impact of policies on gradients. There are many policies that have been implemented in India—including public food distribution, caste-based education policies, village health initiatives, and health insurance expansions—that need to be evaluated in terms of their effects on equity. In addition to these policies targeted at the poor, there is a need

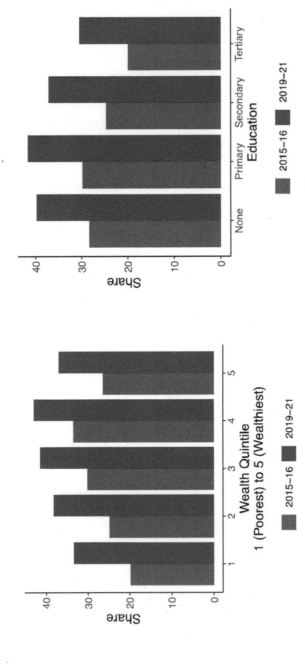

FIGURE 2-5 Enrollment in health insurance program in India, by wealth and education.
SOURCE: Adapted from data in Mohanty et al. (2023, Table 1).

25

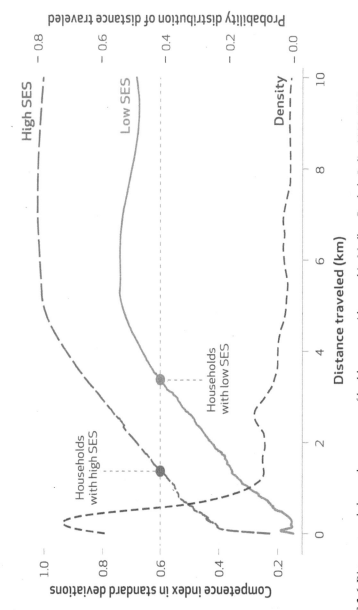

FIGURE 2-6 Distance traveled to and competence of health care providers used in Madhya Pradesh, India, 2009–2011.
NOTE: SES, socioeconomic status.
SOURCE: Das and Mohpal (2016, Exhibit 4). Reprinted with permission.

to evaluate broad population policies that might affect inequality. For example, taxes on sugar or tobacco, or changes to the built environment (e.g., transportation infrastructure, green spaces) could have an effect on existing gradients; there is a need to research these policies to determine their effects.

RESEARCH APPROACHES FOR INEQUALITY

Will Dow (University of California, Berkeley) discussed research approaches for inequality. There are a few key questions to consider for the research agenda in LMICs, said Dow. First, there has been a great deal of research in high-income countries to understand the mechanisms of how inequality affects health. However, what is unknown is whether these mechanisms operate differently in LMICs. Second is the question of how inequality will evolve in different populations. Finally, said Dow, we need to understand what policy approaches will be most effective in addressing inequality. Dow focused his remarks primarily on income inequality and health, but he noted that there are other important factors that impact inequality and health, including the physical and psychological effects of the changing nature of work.

Dow first addressed the mechanisms that link inequality to health by looking at research largely conducted in higher-income countries. Early research documented that countries with higher inequality have worse population health. There are a number of mechanisms that may be at play, said Dow. First, absolute income improves health, but at a diminishing rate. He explained that if two countries have similar average income, but one has higher income inequality, the more unequal country will have more poverty and worse health. Addressing absolute income is important for reducing the effect of inequality on health, he said.

Another mechanism for the link between inequality and health that has been demonstrated in higher-income countries is a psychological one. Segments of the population with lower incomes experience negative psychosocial effects because individuals compare themselves to others with higher income. A third mechanism, said Dow, is social cohesion. In very unequal societies, the more disadvantaged segments have less social capital, and there is less political support for redistributional policies and society-wide health investments. A key question, he said, is how these mechanisms may or may not operate in LMICs with changing economies.

"Inequality has been with us for a long time, and it is going to be with us for a long time," Dow said. He shared a graph that shows the share of global income that goes to the top 10%, middle 40%, and bottom 50% of the population over the past 200 years: see Figure 2-7. However, while inequality has historically been between countries, it is now primarily within countries: see Figure 2-8. This pattern means that it is critical to collect data within countries that include details on individuals across the income spectrum, rather than relying on national averages. Another major change that has occurred is a sharp increase in the female share of labor income because of increased education and rising participation in formal labor markets. Dow said that this is an important area to continue to study; specific foci could include whether the work of women in nonmarket settings is or is not changing and how these trends affect inequality and health.

Income inequality is higher in LMICs, said Dow, with the top 10% of the population earning over half of the national income in many countries, including South Africa, India, and Brazil: see Figure 2-9. With higher inequality in these countries, there is a larger need for policies to address inequality and its associated risks, he said.

Dow discussed three main types of policies aimed at mitigating SES gradients in health: first, taxing the high-income/wealthy segments of the population to fund poverty reduction, which is a "politically difficult proposition in many countries"; second, investing in programs that shift health upward for the entire population; and third, buffering the negative health consequences of low SES by providing interventions to this population. These types of social spending rose dramatically in Europe over the 20th century, with spending on health care, pensions, education, justice, social transfers, and other programs rising from around 10% of gross domestic product (GDP) in 1915 to 45% of GDP in 1980.

While it is difficult to know how each type of expenditure has affected health, the rise of the European welfare state "arguably has had a huge impact on health outcomes in European countries," he said. In contrast, tax revenues and social spending in LMICs are far lower. In sub-Saharan Africa and South and Southeast Asia, tax revenue is under 20% of GDP, and spending on health care and education are less than 3% each. However, there are some LMICs that have been spending much more significantly on social programs. For example, Costa Rica has a very robust social safety net, and it has a smaller SES gradient in health than the United States. Even more striking, said Dow, is the fact that the bottom socioeconomic quartile of the Costa Rican population has better health than the bottom quartile of the U.S. population.

While large public investments are clearly needed in order to make an impact on inequality and health, said Dow, the ability to make these investments is constrained by an ongoing shift from public to private wealth. Over the last 50 years, private wealth has been increasing dramatically in high-income countries, while public wealth—the sum of financial and nonfinancial assets, net of debts, held by governments—has decreased at the same time: see Figure 2-10. Dow said the same trends are occurring in most LMICs, though not yet as dramatically.

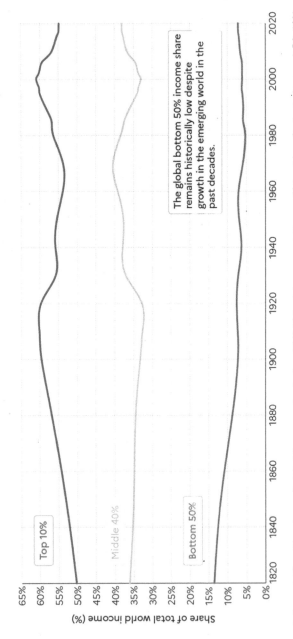

FIGURE 2-7 Global income inequality, 1820–2020.

Interpretation: The share of global income going to top 10% highest incomes at the world level has fluctuated around 50–60% between 1820 and 2020 (50% in 1820, 60% in 1910, 56% in 2000, 61% in 1980, 55% in 2020), while the share going to the bottom 50% lowest incomes has generally been around or below 10% (14% in 1820, 7% in 1910, 5% in 1980, 6% in 2000, 7% in 2020). Global inequality has always been very large. It rose between 1820 and 1910 and shows little long-run trend between 1910 and 2020. **Sources and series:** see wir2022.wid.world/methodology and Chancel and Piketty (2021).

SOURCE: Chancel et al. (2022, Figure 2.1). Reprinted under Creative Commons 4.0 (https://creativecommons.org/licenses/by/4.0/) on behalf of World Inequality Lab, https://inequalitylab.world/en/

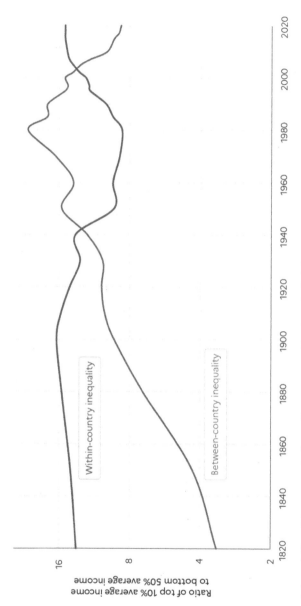

FIGURE 2-8 Between-country and within-country inequality, 1820–2020.

Interpretation: Between-country inequality, as measured by the ratio T10/B50 between the average incomes of the top 10% and the bottom 50% (assuming everybody within a country has the same income), rose between 1820 and 1980 and has since strongly declined. Within-country inequality, as measured also by the ratio T10/B50 between the average incomes of the top 10% and the bottom 50% (assuming all countries have the same average income), rose slightly between 1820 and 1910, declined between 1910 and 1980, and rose since 1980. Income is measured per capita after pensions and unemployement insurance transfers and before income and wealth taxes. ***Sources and series:*** wir2022.wid.world/methodology and Chancel and Piketty (2021).

SOURCE: Chancel et al. (2022, Figure 2.4). Reprinted under Creative Commons 4.0 (https://creativecommons.org/licenses/by/4.0/) on behalf of World Inequality Lab, https://inequalitylab.world/en/

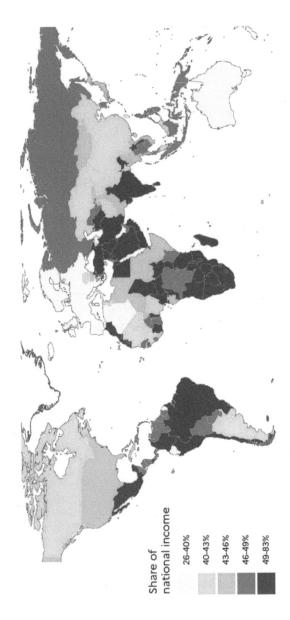

Share of
national income

26-40%

40-43%

43-46%

46-49%

49-83%

Interpretation: *In South Africa, the top 10% captures 67% of total national income, whereas the value is 32% in France. Income is measured after pension and unemployment benefits are received by individuals, but before other taxes they pay and transfers they receive.* ***Sources and series:*** *wir2022.wid.world/methodology.*

FIGURE 2-9 Income inequality across the globe.
SOURCE: Chancel et al. (2022, Figure 1.6a). Reprinted under Creative Commons 4.0 (https://creativecommons.org/licenses/by/4.0/) on behalf of World Inequality Lab, https://inequalitylab.world/en/

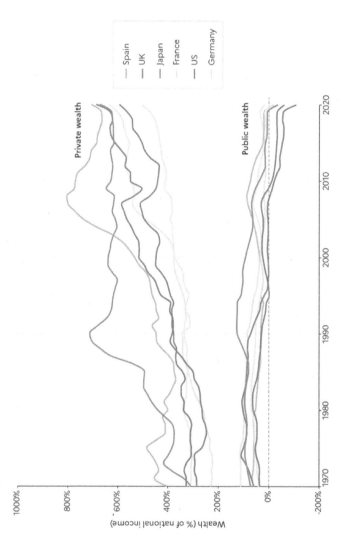

FIGURE 2-10 Shift from public to private wealth, 1970–2020 in select countries.

Interpretation: *In the UK, public wealth dropped from 60% of national income to -106% between 1970 and 2020. Public wealth is the sum of all financial and non-financial assets, net of debts, held by governments. **Sources and series:** wir2022.wid.world/methodology. Bauluz et al. (2021) and updates.*

SOURCE: Chancel et al. (2022, Figure 3.2). Reprinted under Creative Commons 4.0 (https://creativecommons.org/licenses/by/4.0/) on behalf of World Inequality Lab, https://inequalitylab.world/en/

In conclusion, Dow suggested three approaches to research that should be prioritized. First, there is a need to build on cross-national research by using harmonized surveys across LMICs and high-income countries in order to test hypotheses on inequality, health, and policy. This type of research is necessary, he said, because there are not usually "beautiful natural experiments" in which it is easy to see causation between a policy and a health outcome. Second, there is a need for research on specific policy changes or interventions in different LMIC contexts in order to grow the generalizable knowledge base. This will require more investment in LMIC surveys, as well as building research capacity in LMICs. Finally, there is a need for macro-level approaches that capture general equilibrium feedbacks. For example, the National Transfer Accounts project has begun incorporating inequality as an element in order to look at the impacts of demographic dividends and their relationships on changing health in more than 60 countries. This will require more investment in macro-level research and macro-level researchers, said Dow.

DISCUSSION

Following the speakers, Minki Chatterji (National Institute on Aging) moderated a question-and-answer session with speakers and participants. She began by summarizing the sessions' presentations. Inequality remains a problem, and there are implications for health. We have some idea of the causal mechanisms through which inequality leads to adverse health outcomes, including tobacco use, obesity, diabetes, and access to care, Chatterji said. However, these mechanisms are still "a little bit fuzzy," particularly in LMIC contexts. There is a need for research on mechanisms in LMICs, as well as on different policies and how they lead to different outcomes. Chatterji asked panelists to comment on two questions related to these needs. First, why is this research not happening with the data that already exist? Second, are the data and infrastructure in place to do this research, and if not, what is needed?

Avila responded that the answers to these questions vary by country. For example, there are a lot of data for Mexico, but more are needed in other countries. For countries that have significant data, a lot could be learned by linking longitudinal datasets with administrative-level data. One reason that this has not yet been done, she said, is that the data are relatively recent so "we are still kind of catching up."

Sudharsanan offered his perspective from working in India. Administrative data are often not available, are of poor quality, or are difficult to obtain. Even something as basic as data on health care claims do not exist, he said. The lack of data means that researchers have to "let go" of the goal of a comprehensive, "satisfying" micro-causal estimate. He added that the incentives in public health are often geared toward quicker, easier types of research that can "generate ten publications" from one dataset. There is a need, he said, to find ways to reward deeper types of inquiry that take more time.

Dow agreed that it can be very difficult to get access to data, in part because many countries do not have a culture of data sharing. This is beginning to change, but more efforts are needed to encourage and support data sharing. In other countries, in particular in sub-Saharan Africa, the data are simply not available. There is a need to invest in the data that will be necessary to evaluate policy changes. In addition, Dow said that more work is needed on building capacity. He said that the mechanisms for supporting scholars and researchers in LMICs are underdeveloped and frequently not well matched to the needs of the scholars.

Yaohui Zhao (Peking University; workshop planning committee member) agreed with the need for capacity building and said that there is a need to work with countries on what kinds of incentives are provided to researchers. For example, most grants have certain restrictions on how money can be spent, and these restrictions may be in conflict with the constraints and incentives for researchers from certain LMICs. There is a need to align incentives in order to facilitate easier collaboration among researchers across country lines.

3

Conceptual and Methodological Barriers

Key Points Highlighted by the Presenters

- Data from cohort studies, studies with individuals, and natural experiments can allow researchers to better understand and assess the causal impact of early-life experiences on later-life health. **(BELTRÁN-SÁNCHEZ)**

- Most environments in low- and middle-income countries (LMICs) have not been described or investigated with respect to Alzheimer's or other diseases of aging, particularly in rural and informal urban areas. **(CLARK)**

- Generate innovative global aging data that capture diverse aging contexts across and within LMICs to better understand the biosocial aging process of individuals with vastly different life-course experiences. **(KOHLER)**

Ayaga Bawah (University of Ghana, workshop planning committee member) moderated the second session of the workshop focused on identifying new conceptual, theoretical, methodological, and data investments that are needed to move from purely descriptive cross-national analyses to more causal analyses, in order to create a better understanding of how inequality, environmental exposures, and changing family structures affect health and well-being at older ages in low- and middle-income countries (LMICs).

IMPACT OF EARLY CONDITIONS AND BIOLOGICAL CLOCKS

Hiram Beltrán-Sánchez (University of California, Los Angeles) focused his remarks on two methods of research: using cohort studies to look at the impact of early conditions on older adult outcomes and using blood samples to study "biological clocks" in evaluating aging. He used data from Latin American countries to illustrate his points but emphasized that these methods of research would be relevant in many LMICs.

Impact of Early Conditions

Child mortality in Latin American countries has dropped dramatically over the last 100 years, said Beltrán-Sánchez: see Figure 3-1. There were medical, social, and economic changes that occurred during this period that contributed to the decline, but the changes happened at different times and affected different birth cohorts. People born prior to 1935 in Latin America lived in a time with very little medical or public health infrastructure. Between the mid-1930s and the mid-1980s, birth cohorts benefited from the deployment of medical technology and public health campaigns, such as vaccinations and antidiarrheal disease interventions. People born prior to the 1970s were born into families with an average size of 5 or 6 children. In the 1970s, there was a massive decline in fertility, with families shrinking to about two children per woman. Finally, economic improvement occurred in Latin American countries in the late 1980s and early 1990s; birth cohorts born during and after this period benefited from increased economic well-being.

Looking at the later-life outcomes for birth cohorts from different time periods, said Beltrán-Sánchez, allows one to examine whether and how growing up in different conditions affects aging and health outcomes. There are two potential approaches that one could use to examine these data: macro-aggregate research and Mendelian randomization. Macro-aggregate research cannot be used to make causal inferences, but it can allow one to examine descriptively a birth cohort's early conditions and later outcomes. For example, some research shows that improved early conditions may be linked with an increase in morbidity and mortality later in life, as a result of milder mortality selection pressures (Beltrán-Sánchez et al., 2022). In order to understand the causal relationship between an event and health outcomes, it is necessary to conduct micro-level research using individual-level data, said Beltrán-Sánchez. Individual-level data can be used to conduct randomized controlled trials, to use natural experiments to look at the

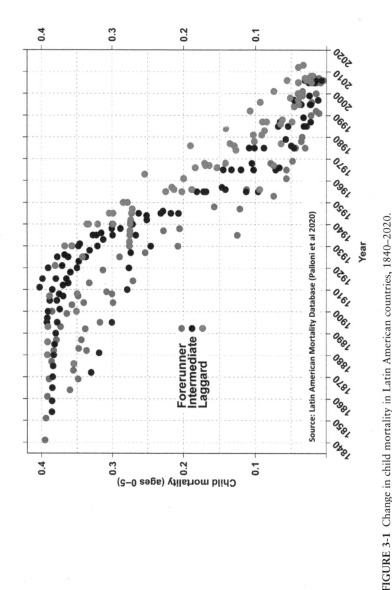

FIGURE 3-1 Change in child mortality in Latin American countries, 1840–2020.
NOTES: Forerunners (blue): Argentina, Costa Rica, Cuba, Uruguay; Laggards (red): Bolivia, El Salvador, Guatemala, Honduras, Nicaragua, Paraguay, Peru; Intermediate (black): Chile, Colombia, Dominican Republic, Ecuador, Mexico, Panama, Venezuela.
SOURCE: Workshop presentation by Hiram Beltrán-Sánchez. Created from data in the Latin American Mortality Database 2, University of Wisconsin System: https://www.ssc.wisc.edu/cdha/latinmortality2/

impact of an event on later outcomes, or to utilize Mendelian randomization[1] to examine the causal effect of an exposure.

Mendelian randomization, he said, is an "extremely exciting and hopefully very useful" approach. It has been more commonly used in epidemiological studies rather than in nationally representative studies, but with the increasing collection of biological data, research can be done that takes account of genetic variation. Beltrán-Sánchez shared an example of his research that used natural experiments to study the impact of events on health outcomes. In 1918, Puerto Rico experienced the worldwide flu pandemic and also had an earthquake-caused tsunami that affected a certain region of the country. Using the variation across regions, Beltrán-Sánchez and his colleagues looked for causal effects of fetal and postnatal exposure to the flu, the tsunami, or both (Palloni et al., 2020).

Biological Clocks

Biological clocks are generally defined as "indicators of accumulated age-related latent physiological change computed with the aid of a battery of biological markers of major physiological domains," said Beltrán-Sánchez. One type of biological clock, the "epiclock," uses epigenetic markers and chronological age (CA; first-generation epiclocks) or may also incorporate blood biomarkers or health behaviors, such as smoking (second-generation epiclocks). Researchers in New Zealand are conducting a cohort study that uses data to compute the "pace of aging," or the rate at which underlying physical deterioration is occurring. These tools can be used to assess how fast people are aging, whether aging is different among populations, and whether the pace is changing over time. Comparing a person's biological age (BA) with their CA can identify individuals with "accelerated aging." That is, individuals whose BAs are older than their CAs are aging faster. Accelerated aging is associated with excess mortality and shorter life expectancy; in contrast, individuals whose BAs are "younger" than their CAs show an increase in life expectancy. Beltrán-Sánchez emphasized that these associations on a population level are not causal but are relevant markers worth examining. In order to find causal determinants of the differences between BA and CA, it would be necessary to collect repeated measures of biological markers from individuals. Collecting biomarkers in the field is "not an easy task," he said, and it is very expensive. Currently, the assays for epigenetic clocks are expensive, but he is hopeful they will become more affordable over time.

---

[1]This term, and its applications, are discussed in detail at https://www.cdc.gov/genomics/events/precision_med_pop.htm

In order to conduct this kind of research, Beltrán-Sánchez said, there is a need for multidisciplinary researchers who understand biology, can make connections with indicators, and are capable of using tools that can determine causation. He emphasized that while individual-level data are important in order to understand causation, "we should not lose sight" of macro-aggregates that are equally important for understanding the connections between life events and health outcomes.

INVESTING IN DATA FOR AGING

All work conducted at the interface of high-income countries and LMICs is "being done against a background of the history we share—colonialism, slavery, exploitation," said Sam Clark (The Ohio State University). Researchers working in this area should keep this in mind and should lean on the work of people in other fields engaging with these topics. Clark gave several examples of work that he recommends:

- *When People Come First: Critical Studies in Global Health* (Biehl & Petryna, 2013);
- *Critical Epidemiology and the People's Health* (Breilh, 2021);
- Epidemiological Accountability: Philanthropists, Global Health, and the Audit of Saving Lives (Reubi, 2018);
- Time to Take Critical Race Theory Seriously: Moving Beyond a Colour-Blind Gender Lens in Global Health (Yam et al., 2021); and
- Decolonizing Global Health: What Should Be the Target of this Movement and Where Does It Lead? (Kwete et al., 2022)

Clark explained that his background and training are in biology, engineering, and demography. Earlier in his career, he worked on health and demographic surveillance sites in Africa, with an emphasis on data collection, data management, and data analysis. More recently, he has been working to develop a new method for estimating under-5 mortality; UNICEF now uses this method for their global estimates. Currently, he said, he has been developing a "verbal autopsy" to estimate the population burden of disease.[2] This process has involved developing global standards, creating new statistical methods for automated analysis of the data, and working to move verbal autopsy out of the research setting and into the normal infrastructure of ministries of health and national statistical systems. A new component, he said, has been adding minimally invasive tissue samples to a

---

[2]For a definition of verbal autopsy and current uses, see https://www.who.int/standards/classifications/other-classifications/verbal-autopsy-standards-ascertaining-and-attributing-causes-of-death-tool

verbal autopsy and building a reference death archive in order to use these data to calibrate machine learning methods.

When trying to determine cause and effect in aging and health outcomes, there are multiple influences on outcomes and different data sources and methods for each of them. Diseases are complicated, and they are affected by biology, behavior, the environment, and society; each of these influences also interacts with the others. Biology interacts with behavior and environment over the life course, in the context of society, to create disease outcomes. Clark then discussed each of these areas in turn, looking at the objective of the research, what specifically is being studied, and how cause and effect can be determined.

Research on biology aims to find biological mechanisms to explain how molecules affect one another, eventually resulting in outcomes at the cellular, organ, or person level. This research can be conducted by looking at molecules, individual humans, or population-level genetics. Cause and effect are established through experiments, although Clark noted that most experiments are conducted on cell lines or animal models, rather than humans. Research on biology is largely generalizable and transferable because biological mechanisms are generally deterministic and predictable. One example of biological research in the aging space, said Clark, is research on alleles of the apolipoprotein E gene and how they contribute to Alzheimer's risk.

Behavioral research seeks to determine how individual behaviors increase or decrease the risk of disease, its progression, and the outcomes. This research looks at individual humans and groups of humans and establishes cause and effect through observational studies and various forms of randomized studies. Clark said that evidence from behavioral research is sometimes generalizable and transferable since some humans share behaviors, but there are nuanced differences. Measurement of behavior can be challenging, he said; it is affected by circumstances and the quality of interactions (e.g., interviews, participant observation). Clark noted that measuring behavior in LMICs can be particularly challenging: researchers and participants each come to the work with their own view of the world and their understanding of how things happen. Each party may be "operating with quite a different cognitive structure," which can affect how questions are asked, what participants say, and how researchers understand what is said.

Research on environmental factors, whether at the biological or sociocultural level, is very important, said Clark. While "environment" can be defined in many different ways, Clark focused on the physical environment. This type of research would look at how the physical environment (e.g., pollution) affects disease dynamics and individual disease outcomes. Cause and effect are established through a combination of observational studies and experiments, both intentional and accidental. Accidental—or natural—experiments such as natural disasters can present excellent opportunities to learn more about cause and effect. Measurement can be both deterministic and precise, he said, and also use statistical estimates involving distributions, uncertainty, and confidence. The generalizability of this research depends on the nature of the environmental factor, said Clark: biological factors in the environment are more generalizable than sociocultural factors.

Population-level epidemiology is a type of research that seeks to provide population-level descriptions of the burden of disease, disease dynamics, and cause and effect. The subject of such research is well defined, generally covering large populations of human beings, and essential measures include the prevalence and incidence of disease. Cause and effect can be established through observational or randomized studies. Epidemiology describes or infers how many people are affected, where they live, when they are affected, and who they are, said Clark. This work can be done at various levels of granularity, although in some areas, there is a lack of even population-level data, let alone the ability to disaggregate further. Epidemiological evidence is usually population and circumstance specific, so it is difficult to generalize. Findings are most often statistical in nature—for example, estimates of distributions and uncertainty.

Clark then described each of these types of research in the context of the state of research in LMICs and what is needed. Biological research can largely be "borrowed" from high-income countries, he said, but there is a need to replicate these findings in LMICs to ensure that they hold across contexts. In addition, there is a need to develop and expand the ability to conduct research with biomarkers, animal models, and cell lines in these settings. Unlike biological research, behavioral research is largely not generalizable, and much work needs to be done in LMICs. Behavior is contextual and cultural, thus research must be done in LMIC settings and in a way that accounts for the sociocultural and contextual circumstances of LMICs. Clark emphasized that cultures and languages must be handled carefully, and Western medical concepts cannot be directly transferred to many LMIC contexts.

Most environments in LMICs have not been described or investigated with respect to diseases of aging, including Alzheimer's. This is particularly true, he said, for people who live in rural areas or informal urban areas (e.g., settlements on the periphery of cities). There is much to do in the area of environmental research, said Clark, such as setting up environmental monitoring stations and linking this information with survey and other data. Like environmental research, epidemiological research is lacking in rural and informal urban areas. In many LMICs, the burden of diseases of aging has not been directly measured, other than in special populations. There are a number of research needs in this area:

- describing the basic burden of disease;
- increasing coverage to whole populations;
- creating measurement systems with the ability to operate at fine(r) levels of granularity;
- longitudinal surveillance; and
- routine, population-scale, continuous monitoring.

Clark closed by identifying ways that research in LMICs can be improved and increased. First, he said, there is a need to train researchers in these countries. A lack of trained individuals is the "number one impediment" to improving research, he said. Training is needed in a variety of areas, including surveys, trials, and research design; electronic data capture; data management; data ethics; Bayesian statistics, machine learning, and general (frequentist) statistics; sample design; and longitudinal research design. Second, global health needs to be decolonized; this will lead to better, "more context-relevant research that has a higher chance of driving meaningful change," he said. Third, there is a need for public, open-access funding for researcher-initiated projects and to facilitate partnerships between scientists in high-income countries and those in LMICs. It is important, he said, to avoid foundation-driven work that narrowly adheres to the foundation's view of what should be done. Finally, Clark said, new data, methods, and approaches are needed that are adapted to LMIC settings. Work in this area could include:

- building basic surveillance into routine administrative systems;
- leveraging existing data and finding new ways to use them;
- building on health and demographic surveillance systems; and
- designing and building longitudinal monitoring systems that use vital statistics, surveys, and health and demographic surveillance data.

All of this work, said Clark, will require cross-trained individuals and interdisciplinary teams. Building capacity within LMICs to design, conduct, analyze, and translate research is an essential part of improving understanding of aging and health in these countries.

GLOBAL AGING DATA

Hans Peter Kohler (University of Pennsylvania) began his presentation by noting that there is tremendous variation within and across LMICs, in economic development, mortality patterns, and demographics, among other characteristics. Understanding aging across these contexts requires identifying and acknowledging the major contextual differences within and across LMICs. For example, among the countries that were the poorest in the 1950s, some have developed rapidly and are now relatively affluent; others have developed more slowly; and others, such as Malawi, have remained quite poor, he said: see Figure 3-2. In addition, individuals age against a backdrop of disease and mortality that affects survival; when we study older individuals, "we study survivors."

Kohler noted that there have been major shifts in mortality within and across LMICs. For example, under-5 mortality in Malawi was around 35% in 1950, and the HIV epidemic raised mortality for adults. Today's older adults are "very resilient," having survived high mortality across the life course. The patterns and shifts in mortality have an impact on many of the outcomes that aging researchers are interested in. Demographically, the populations of LMICs are aging at different rates, which affects the context in which individuals age. For example, Malawi and South Africa have very different population pyramids, with projections showing a larger proportion of older South Africans by 2050: see Figure 3-3. Within and across LMICs, individuals are aging in "strikingly different contexts," and researchers need to make the effort to identify and understand these differences and to capture the diversity of aging.

Most of the current knowledge about aging comes from research in high-income countries, said Kohler. One question is whether this knowledge is generalizable to LMICs and whether patterns observed in high-income countries hold for LMICs. A related question, he said, is whether there are things that can be learned about successful aging in LMICs that could shed light on the challenges of aging in high-income countries. Furthering understanding of aging in LMICs has the potential to inform interventions, policies, and programs in both LMICs and high-income countries.

Kohler shared additional data from Malawi to illustrate how research on aging in a low-resource environment might be useful in other contexts. In Malawi, there is a great deal of heterogeneity in health and aging, but individuals can be categorized into three subsets: one subset has had persistently poor mental and physical health through adulthood and into older age; another subset had good health during adulthood but their health rapidly declined as they reached older ages; and one small subset has maintained good health throughout adulthood and into older age: see Figure 3-4. In other contexts, said Kohler, one might assume that the third subset had better access to resources than others, but this study population was uniformly poor. The individuals who maintained better health, he said, tended to be "very resourceful in utilizing the knowledge, the resources, and the health care access" they needed in order to accomplish relatively

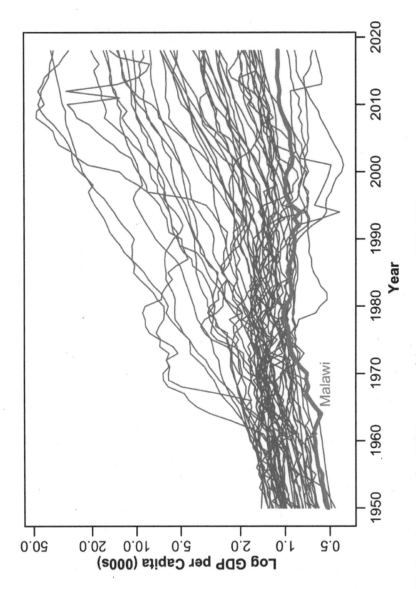

FIGURE 3-2 Gross domestic product (GDP) per capita of the poorest countries, 1950–2018.
SOURCE: Ciancio et al. (2023, Figure 1a). Reprinted with permission.

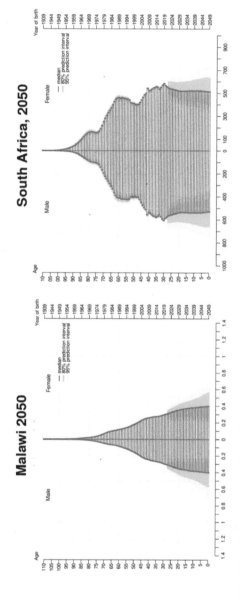

FIGURE 3-3 Population projections in Malawi and South Africa, 2050.
SOURCE: Workshop presentation by Hans Kohler based on data from U.N. World Population Prospects: http://population.un.org/wpp/. Data reused under Creative Commons license 3.0 IGO: http://creativecommons.org/licenses/by/3.0/igo/

successful aging. Similar patterns have been seen in cognitive aging, with a small group of individuals being more resilient to decline. Understanding this variation and teasing apart the driving factors of resiliency is critical to understanding the aging process in both LMICs and other countries.

One factor that is somewhat unique to LMICs, said Kohler, is the widespread exposure to early-life adversity. People in LMICs experience many more shocks—such as famines, wars, and natural disasters—than people in high-income countries. A number of researchers have studied whether these early-life shocks have later-life effects, and what these effects are. For example, birth cohorts that were affected in utero by a 1949 famine in Malawi have slightly better cardiovascular health in older ages. Kohler noted that this is contrary to other research that has found negative effects from early-life adversity. Kohler and his colleagues are looking for mechanisms by which adversity can translate into better health outcomes; they theorize that adversity may have epigenetic effects on resilience.

Given the complexities of aging and the variety of contexts in which people age, Kohler said that it is critical to create conceptual frameworks that facilitate integration of findings across different contexts. He shared a framework that guides him and his colleagues in their work in Malawi: see Figure 3-5. The framework contains a number of innovations that allow the researchers to measure and study a wide range of factors, including the genome, epigenome, physiological and neurological systems, the brain and other organs, and biochemical messengers. These biological mechanism data can be integrated with information about social context and individual risk factors in order to better understand aging and why some individuals age "faster" or "slower." Kohler noted that it is important to design studies that allow for causal inference when appropriate. However, he cautioned, researchers must be cognizant of the context in which they are working and aware of their impact. For example, a study conducted in 2004 examined whether mortality was affected by knowledge of one's HIV status. All participants were tested for HIV status but only those who chose to learn the result were told of their status. Those who learned in the course of the study that they were HIV positive were less likely to survive the next few years. "Telling individuals that they have a fatal disease" at a time and place that antiretroviral treatment was not available produced behaviors that reduced their survival, said Kohler.

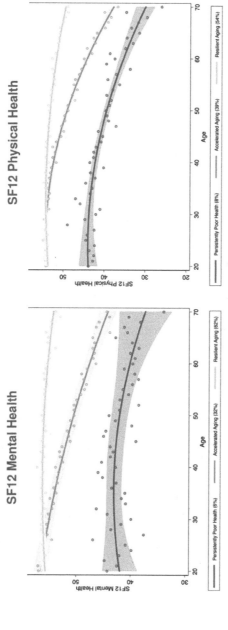

FIGURE 3-4 Trajectories of health across the life course in Malawi.
SOURCE: Hoang et al. (2023, Figures 3a and 3b). Reprinted with permission.

48

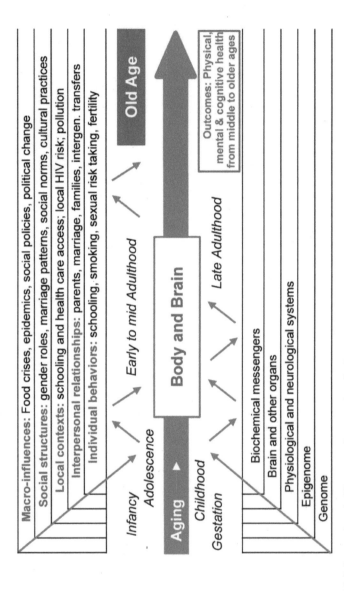

FIGURE 3-5 Innovations in life-course frameworks of aging.
SOURCE: Hoang et al. (2023, Figure 2). Reprinted with permission.

Kohler closed by offering his ideas of what data and methods innovations are needed in order to expand and improve research on aging in LMICs:

- creating innovative global aging data that capture diverse aging contexts across and within LMICs;
- allowing life-course analyses that include family and community contexts;
- capturing biological, social, and behavioral aspects of aging;
- allowing comparative analyses via harmonization of key outcomes and exposures, while recognizing limitations of doing so across LMICs;
- capturing changing environmental, social, and economic contexts;
- aspiring to be nationally representative, while utilizing special datasets (e.g., existing longitudinal cohort studies, demographic and health surveillance sites) that offer unique opportunities;
- documenting distinctive and common aging trajectories across the socioeconomic development spectrum;
- leveraging diversity of global aging contexts to enhance understanding of aging processes;
- planning research design to allow for causal analyses while recognizing the ongoing need for insightful descriptive analyses; and
- building strong partnerships and inclusive research teams.

DISCUSSION

Continuing the question-and-answer discussion from the previous session (see Chapter 2), panelists and participants considered approaches for building researcher capacity in LMICs. Jennifer Ailshire (University of Southern California) said that in her work with predoctoral and postdoctoral students, a major challenge is that many of the students interested in studying aging are foreign students who are ineligible to be included in training grants from the National Institutes of Health (NIH). While changing the training grant system may not be possible, Ailshire suggested that there could be a system for supplementing NIH training grants to allow for these foreign students. There are "phenomenal training opportunities in the United States," and there is a need to work with global partners to enhance the support available to students from LMICs, she said.

Nikkil Sudharsanan (Technical University of Munich) added that in Germany, there are a number of government programs designed explicitly to bring researchers from LMICs to Germany for training. These programs are "transformative," and it would be great if the United States could do something similar.

Rebeca Wong (University of Texas Medical Branch at Galveston; planning committee chair) said that while she supports the idea of programs for LMIC scholars, it is important to ensure that these efforts do not "crowd out" scholars in the United States. She added that improving support for LMIC scholars should be done on a high, country-to-country level, rather than through individual efforts. For example, national science organizations could work together to provide scholarships and incentives for researcher training.

Mary Ganguli (University of Pittsburgh; workshop planning committee member) shared a training model that could serve as an example to follow. The Global Brain Health Institute sponsors fellows from around the world; fellows are paired with a mentor and spend a year in Dublin or San Francisco learning about brain health and dementia. The idea of the program, she said, is that the fellows will return to their home countries to work. Interestingly, the most difficult thing has been finding housing that students from poorer countries can afford. Ganguli also mentioned the importance of aligning training with the incentives and timelines in the trainees' home countries. For example, she said, potential trainees in India turned down a training opportunity because they would pass the age of eligibility for government service if they participated. "We have to think about the career opportunities and career tracks within the countries when we offer these things," she said.

4

Research and Policy Interventions

Key Points Highlighted by the Presenters

- Taking a life-course approach to aging allows researchers to learn more about how early-life experiences and exposures affect health and well-being later in life. (**PAYNE**)

- There are major challenges related to generalizability and transportability of findings of research in low- and middle-income countries (LMICs); however, there are opportunities to use findings on subgroups or specific populations. (**CANNING**)

- Current evidence on the role of social policies to promote healthy aging in LMICs is robust yet scarce; research priorities include the further development of data infrastructure and methodologies to strengthen causal identification, external validity, and transportability of findings. (**KOBAYASHI**)

The third session of the workshop focused on research and policy interventions. Session presenters had been asked to discuss how research in low- and middle-income countries (LMICs) can create a better understanding of how different social environments and public policies influence health outcomes related to aging and provide lessons that can be used in other settings, including the United States. Presenters had also been asked to consider what kinds of policy interventions, such as those related to pensions, long-term care, and formal and informal care, can influence the health and the well-being of older populations in LMICs.

CONTEXTUAL DETERMINANTS OF FUNCTIONAL HEALTH AND DISABILITY

There is a huge amount of heterogeneity in LMICs, said Collin Payne (Australian National University). This heterogeneity means that there is an opportunity to learn how different contexts, economic situations, and policies can affect health and aging. However, it also presents a challenge because it can be difficult to draw strong conclusions from scattered evidence and to understand how evidence from one country can translate to another. Payne focused his presentation on several themes that he has identified in recent literature:

- functional health across different contexts;
- development and trends in health over time;
- met and unmet needs for care;
- moving beyond population-level approaches—social inequalities in LMICs;
- policy changes and health; and
- determinants of disability.

He discussed each of these in turn.

There is a clear relationship between economic development and mortality, Payne said, but the relationship between economic development and functional health is less clear. Recent studies in LMICs have found no clear relationship between economic development and disability-free life expectancy (DFLE; Prina et al., 2020). Payne's own research found that DFLE is not substantially different between the United States and a set of Latin American countries, despite wide economic differences (Payne, 2018). While the absolute number of older adults with limitations in LMICs will grow massively in the next 30 years, he said, it is unclear whether and how economic development in these countries will affect disability and DFLE. There is substantial variation among LMICs that cannot be explained by national-level measures of economic development; more research is needed to understand how social context and policies might be influencing these differences.

Payne noted that many presenters have already touched on the issue of early-life conditions and health later in life. More research is needed to understand how life-course exposure to rapid social, contextual, and policy changes shapes health among older adults in LMICs. Research has found that changes in life conditions may lead to changes in successive birth cohorts' risk of obesity, diabetes, and mortality (Beltrán-Sánchez et al., 2022;

Palloni & Beltrán-Sánchez, 2017). One "troubling" finding is that cohorts that grow up in relatively more developed conditions end up with worse health than older cohorts. Studies have found an expansion of morbidity occurring over cohorts in Mexico (Payne & Wong, 2019), as well as among less advantaged groups in the United States (Payne, 2022). In China, research found that the socioeconomic status of adults plays a substantial role in shaping healthy longevity. It is critical, said Payne, to look at the full life course and the exposures that happen over time in order to better understand their impact on older age health, disability, and mortality.

As older adults age in LMICs, they will need care. The question, said Payne, is how these needs for functional health support will match up with available care. Unmet needs are determined by complex factors that are connected to development, family structure, and institutional supports. When institutional support is not available, the availability and capacity of others is hugely important. Who cares for adults and the quality of this care matter for meeting care needs. There are some indications, said Payne, that unmet needs may be higher among "younger-old" people with physical limitations (Brinkmann et al., 2021; Harling et al., 2020). These individuals might not "fit the mold" of who is expected to need care, but attention is needed to ensure that this population is not left behind.

Inequalities within and among LMICs are an interesting area that has often been overlooked, said Payne. Some research has shown that inequalities in health are greater in high-income countries than in low-income countries. For example, inequality in disability by income is much greater in high-income countries (Li et al., 2023), and mortality gradients by education, wealth, and occupation were lower in middle-income countries as compared with high-income ones in the Asia-Pacific area (Xu et al., 2023). Payne noted that effective health care systems may affect inequalities in LMICs (Rosero-Bixby & Dow, 2016).

One policy change that has been studied quite a bit in LMICs is the introduction of public health insurance. Many countries have implemented national health care schemes in the last several decades, with varying levels of success. However, said Payne, there is lots of heterogeneity in how national health insurance reforms are designed, which makes direct comparisons across countries difficult (Lagomarsino et al., 2012). The available evidence does suggest that insurance has led to increased utilization of care; however, the effects on treatment and health outcomes are unclear (Erlangga et al., 2019; Limwattananon et al., 2017; Parker et al., 2018; Rivera-Hernandez et al., 2016).

Payne said that one area that is ripe for further research is the determinants of disability in LMICs. Rather than simply looking at cross-national differences of functional health, one needs to understand why these differences exist. Research has found that chronic disease plays a large role in disability. One cross-sectional analysis in 11 countries found dementia to be a major factor, and two-thirds of disability was associated with chronic diseases (Sousa et al., 2009). Diabetes is also a major contributor: studies in Mexico and South Africa found large losses in life expectancy and DFLE among people with diabetes (Andrade, 2010; Payne et al., 2023). In fact, a study in South Africa found that the losses of life expectancy and DFLE were larger for diabetes than for HIV. These findings are especially pertinent given the rising rates of diabetes and the poor state of diabetes care in many LMICs, he said.

In terms of improving and expanding research on aging in LMICs—and ensuring that research findings are helpful for developing policy—Payne identified five priority areas for action:

1. measurement and comparability;
2. the role of policy in shaping later life health;
3. noncommunicable diseases and care as a determinant of population health;
4. life-course exposures at micro and macro levels; and
5. translating findings to other contexts.

He discussed each of these in turn.

Researchers who are working across countries often seek to use the same measures so that results can be compared. Payne said that while comparability is beneficial, they need to consider whether measures developed in high-income countries are serving the needs of LMICs. For example, subjective and objective measures of health often do not closely align in LMICs (Capistrant et al., 2014; Payne, 2018). One study found that accounting for physical performance rather than subjective measures leads old-age dependency ratios to increase in LMICs and decline in high-income countries (Kämpfen et al., 2020). Payne said there is a constant balancing of interpretability and measurement and simplicity and complexity. One way to address this tension may be to approach "health" from multiple angles rather than looking at each facet in isolation.

There is relatively limited research on the relationship between macro-level policy changes and micro-level well-being in later life. There is evidence on how policies have affected health behaviors and health care access, but far less evidence about how they have affected health itself, he said. It is challenging to study policies cross-nationally because of the complexities of policies and the contexts in which they are implemented. Payne noted that the Social PoLicy Archive for SHARE (SPLASH) database[1] for social policy researchers in Europe is an "amazing resource"; a similar shared database

---

[1] SPLASH: https://share-eric.eu/data/data-set-details/social-policy-archive-for-share-splash

would be a "huge boon" for researchers working in LMICs who want to understand the role of policy in their work.

Noncommunicable diseases are a major determinant of health in aging in LMICs, said Payne, but there is a question as to whether the right data exist to inform policy. Studies on disease in LMICs tend to ask questions in slightly different ways, which makes comparability very difficult. Noncommunicable diseases are increasingly a major determinant of late-life well-being in LMICs, he said, so it is essential that one can measure disease and outcomes in order to assess how health systems are (or are not) keeping up with the challenges, and that measures are comparable across contexts. There is a need to collect both micro- and macro-level data about individual health conditions and how individuals are interacting with health care systems.

Studies on older adults tend to collect information about education, wealth, housing status, and other factors, and look at how it relates to health. However, Payne said, it is critical to look at the entire life courses of older adults in order to understand how changes and development have affected population health. For example, he said, in looking at disability, one could compare obesity with changing food systems and diets in LMICs. Life history surveys should be incorporated into more Health and Retirement Study (HRS) International Family of Studies; this would provide a "huge wealth" of detailed information on people's lives as they reach older age. One use of this information would be to allow for retroactive investigation of how policies affect long-term health. In addition to expanded research, Payne said, better theories are needed of how social inequalities emerge and change alongside economic and political development.

As other presenters have noted, Payne said, research in LMICs may be able to inform our knowledge of aging in other contexts by improving understanding of what relationships are contextual, and what relationships are causal. For example, social inequalities in health in many LMICs do not align with those in high-income countries. There are likely many relationships that have been established in high-income countries that do not translate to LMICs, and further research is needed to understand how and why. Payne suggested that understanding whether LMIC findings are generalizable to other contexts will require replicating findings in other geographical areas, social contexts, and levels of development in order to build the evidence base.

GENERALIZATION AND TRANSPORTABILITY

There is a great deal of really interesting research on aging happening in LMICs, including research on biomarkers, the influence of life-course exposures, and the impact of policy, said David Canning (Harvard University). Most of this research has good internal validity: studies with randomization, regression discontinuity, and long follow-up times all help ensure that findings are accurate. However, there are challenges when it comes to external validity, that is, the ability to generalize to the population and transport findings to other populations and contexts. This is problematic, he said, because international comparisons can be very useful for learning more about a given factor and its impact on health. For example, research on the effects of pensions on health in South Africa has found positive effects on health; similar effects were found in rural China. Finding a causal relationship requires a large sample size and a lot of variability in exposure, he said. More data with more variation allows for more information about potential relationships; looking across multiple different countries, with their different contexts and policies, increases the chances of finding a true relationship between a factor and a health outcome. Some countries, such as India, China, and the United States, have a lot of variation in policy across provinces and states, which can be useful for studying the impact of different policies in similar contexts.

There are three assumptions needed for external validity, said Canning: (1) conditional exchangeability, (2) selection positivity, and (3) stable unit treatment value. Conditional exchangeability is necessary for generalizability, or the ability to apply the findings from a sample to the larger population. Conditional exchangeability means that the study sample and the target population have the same distribution of unobserved effect modifiers. In a random sample, the expected distribution would be the same across the sample and the population. This assumption is testable, said Canning. While it may not be possible to identify and correct for all effect modifiers, it is possible to test for parameter equality across a sample and the population. One way of doing so is to make predictions from the sample data and then check if they hold true in the population data. For example, based on mortality data from an internally valid study, is the predicted mortality rate in the population borne out in the macro data?

Selection positivity means that every type of person who is in the population has to be in the sample, that is, have a "positive probability of selection," Canning said. If some segments of a population are not represented, "you have really no hope of generalizing to them." With a random sample, selection positivity is straightforward. With a nonrandom sample, there are ways to test the sample to ensure it is representative and adjust the sample if not.

Canning explained that stable unit treatment value assumption means that what happens in the study sample and in the general population is the same, and that the effects are the same. Harmonization across countries is possible if the measured exposures and outcomes are the same. However, there is an assumption being made that being in the study does not affect the outcome. This is "incredibly problematic," said Canning, because there is evidence that there can be effects from being in a study. For example, people that learn health information due to participation in a study may change their behaviors or health care decisions. Even just being asked questions in a study may have an effect, he said, by making people more sensitive to and aware of health issues. Many studies use a panel design, in which the same group of participants is measured over time. While this design has many benefits for internal validity, it presents challenges for external validity if the panel becomes more dissimilar from the population over waves. This can be accounted for, however, by either comparing the panel with new cross sections over time or by creating a control group to compare with the treatment group. The control group is made up of individuals who are eligible for the study but randomly not selected.

For transportability, or the ability to apply the findings to a new population, Canning said that it is important to look at effect heterogeneity and effect modifiers. Effects are heterogeneous across individuals, and while average population effects may not be the same in different settings, individual effects could be similar. Canning noted that transporting findings from LMICs to the United States as a whole may be too difficult. However, it may be possible to make comparisons with populations that are similar. For example, low-income people in the United States are wealthier than low-income people in LMICs, but the effects of a policy or intervention could be similar. Other groups for which findings could potentially be transportable include HIV-positive populations, migrants from LMICs, and people who experienced early-life adversities.

RESEARCH INFORMING SOCIAL POLICY

Social protection policies that support the economic health and well-being of the most vulnerable populations are critically important, said Lindsay Kobayashi (University of Michigan). These policies have been expanding across the world in recent decades, with more than 130 countries using cash transfers as part of their social protection policies. However, evidence on the relationship between these policies and health remains nascent, she said, for four reasons. First, there is a lack of high-quality data: large population-based samples and longitudinal studies are needed in order to measure pre- and post-policy implementation outcomes. Second, there needs to be variation across different variables so that one can measure heterogeneous treatment effects and subgroup effects. The HRS International Family of Studies are a great starting place, said Kobayashi, but more is needed. The third reason is the challenge of causal identification. Policy change is "very messy" in the real world, and it is difficult to find a valid instrument or source of exogenous variation in exposure to a policy change. Finally, transportability is a big challenge: transporting effect estimates across LMICs or between LMICs and high-income countries is difficult because of big contextual differences. However, she said, she agreed with Canning that there may be opportunities for group transportability.

Despite all these challenges, there is some promising empirical evidence from South Africa and other settings on the effects of social policies on older adults' health. Kobayashi shared data from her work in this area. South Africa has a "really robust" set of social protection policies; the largest are the old-age pension and the child support grant. Between 2008 and 2010, the pension part of the program expanded for men aged 65 and older to those aged 60 and older. Between 2003 and 2012, the upper age limit for the child part of the program, which is targeted at caregivers of young children (the vast majority of whom are mothers), was expanded from 7 to 18.

In investigating the impact of these policy expansions on cognitive health among older adults, Kobayashi and her colleagues (Kobayashi et al., 2021) found that men who benefited from the expansion of the old-age pension had better cognitive function than predicted, based on trends in the cohort of men who did not benefit from the expansion, said Kobayashi. Depending on their age at the time of expansion, different cohorts had an additional 1–5 years of pension over the transition time period. The data revealed a dose–response relationship: men with 5 years of additional eligibility benefited the most. Researchers tested these findings against a negative control group of women of the same age who were not eligible for pension expansion. Kobayashi explained that this comparison was done in order to ensure that the observed effect was not the result of birth cohort or other differences. There was no association, she said, which enhanced the robustness of the original finding.

Women who benefited from the expansion of the child support grant also showed improved cognitive health. Researchers compared eligible women with women who were not eligible but who had children of similar ages. She noted that the positive effect was not seen in women who had five or more children, but that this could be because of imprecise estimation (Kobayashi et al., 2021).

Kobayashi shared another study (Rosenberg et al., 2023) that was designed to look at the impact of cash transfers on HIV incidence among young women; the unique design of the study allowed for an examination of the impact of cash transfers on older adults' cognitive health. She explained that the study provided cash to a randomized sample of households, and a large proportion of these households included an older adult member who eventually was enrolled in Health and Aging in Africa: A Longitudinal Study in South Africa (HAALSI).[2] The overlap between the HIV study and HAALSI provided a unique opportunity to look at the relationship between cash transfers and memory function. On average, individuals from households that were randomized to the cash transfer arm of the study had a slower rate of memory decline than individuals from non–cash transfer households. The effect was strong, said Kobayashi, with a difference of about 0.15 standard deviations over the 6-year period. This provides "really robust evidence" for a casual effect of improved income on protecting memory as individuals age.

In closing, Kobayashi identified three areas to prioritize for future research. First, there is a need for improved data infrastructure on aging in LMICs. This will require longitudinal population-based data on health outcomes. It is "incredibly important" to continue to support the HRS International Family of Studies network, she said. Data are needed to support evaluations of external validity to general populations—without a well-enumerated sampling frame, it is difficult to establish external validity for the purposes of translating findings into policy. Kobayashi agreed with Payne that researchers need comprehensive and publicly available data on social policies (e.g., SPLASH). This is "really high-priority, low-hanging fruit" that would greatly enhance research. A publicly available database with comprehensive information on different types of social protection policies across LMICs would be very valuable and is a "tractable action step."

Kobayashi's second priority area for future research is to focus on key health outcomes, including dementia, cardiometabolic outcomes, disability, and functional capacity. It is critical to look at inequalities in these outcomes, which may play out differently across settings, and how policies can affect inequalities.

Finally, Kobayashi said there is a need for methodological work to strengthen causal identification, external validity, and transportability. This work is "absolutely essential" for appropriate policy translation, so it is important to get it right. Kobayashi noted, however, that transportability is difficult, requiring data on effect-modifying variables in both samples in a study, which is sometimes not possible or desirable. Causal identification and internal validity should "come first."

DISCUSSION

Following the presentations, Minki Chatterji (National Institute on Aging [NIA]) moderated a question-and-answer session. She began by emphasizing her concern about transportability of findings, noting that one purpose for NIA-funded research is to apply evidence from one area to an-

---

[2] https://haalsi.org/

other. Kobayashi responded that transportability is not as big an issue as it may seem. There are many analytical purposes for data that do not require transportability, she said, and research helps to build a cohesive evidence base. There are many general lessons that can be learned from research in one setting that can likely be applied to many other settings—for example, the effectiveness of cash transfers.

Chatterji also commented on the idea for a social policy research database, similar to SPLASH. She wondered about the scale of the task and where and how it could be appropriate to start. Kobayashi suggested that beginning with countries in the HRS International Family of Studies network could be a good starting place and that it could be important to partner with governments in order to fully understand the policies and how they are implemented. Payne agreed with the need for partnerships, saying that partnering with government statistical organizations and other agencies would "go a long way." He said that there is no need to reinvent the wheel, but, instead, researchers can build on networks that already exist. Lisa Berkman (Harvard University) added that while cross-country policy comparisons can be quite complicated, there are many opportunities to compare policies within countries. For example, data can be collected before and after the implementation of a policy, and some policies vary across states or regions in a country. A workshop participant suggested that, in addition to studying the effects of intentional government policies, it could be worthwhile to study how indirect actions or events can affect population health. For example, government regulation of markets and subsidization of certain products could have big implications for health (e.g., increase in obesity and diabetes associated with subsidization of high-calorie foods).

5

The Role of Family

Key Points Highlighted by the Presenters:

- To implement effective policies, data that are high quality, longitudinal, and harmonized are needed across low- and middle-income countries (LMICs). **(IBARRARÁN)**

- The decline in intergenerational coresidence and decreasing numbers of children does not necessarily imply a decrease in family support for older adults and needs to be understood within the broader context of social connectedness and the quality of family relationships. **(CHEN)**

- In Latin America, adults are living longer, but there is a significant gap between life expectancy and health-adjusted life expectancy. **(GARCÍA-PEÑA)**

The fourth session of the workshop was moderated by Emily Agree (Johns Hopkins University, workshop planning committee member) and focused on how family changes might affect the health and well-being of older populations in low- and middle-income countries (LMICs). Specifically, presenters had been asked to consider how changes in household composition, family size, and time to marriage affect the health of older populations.

CARE OF OLDER ADULTS IN LATIN AMERICA

There are three trends in the care environment in Latin American countries, said Pablo Ibarrarán (Inter-American Development Bank [IDB]). First, there is a strong reliance on family care. This is in part because of cultural reasons and in part out of necessity because of a lack of formal care systems. A huge majority of care—around 90%—is done within families, and mostly by women in the family. The second trend, he said, is that the number of older people is increasing because of birth patterns and longer life expectancy. In addition, a higher proportion of older adults are needing care because of the prevalence of chronic diseases that are associated with functional dependency. Third, changes in family size and composition mean that the supply of traditional caregivers is decreasing. A trend toward smaller families and women working in the formal labor market mean that there are fewer available caregivers at the same time that there is an increase in the demand for care.

Professional care is very uncommon in Latin American countries. Only about 0.5% of older people in the region live in long-term institutions, and around 80% of older people being cared for at home are cared for by family members. While data on care are lacking in many countries, said Ibarrarán, data from Argentina show that only 3% of people receiving care at home receive care from someone who is professionally trained. Between two-thirds and three-quarters of care in the home is provided by women. Many women are combining paid work and care work, which has both economic and health consequences. For example, if a woman reduces her paid work in order to care for a family member, she is reducing her potential social security or pension. This has "long-lasting impacts," said Ibarrarán.

Care needs are increasing in Latin America, with about 14.4% of people over 65 being care dependent. With expected demographic changes, the number of people who need care is projected to triple by 2050: see Figure 5-1. This is a conservative estimate, Ibarrarán said, because it assumes the same rate of dependency as today. While care needs are increasing, he reiterated, the supply of caregivers is shrinking. Lower fertility rates, coupled with national and international migration patterns, mean that families are smaller and older people are more likely to live alone. These trends put the traditional care model, which the region has relied on for years, under stress.

These patterns—an increase in care needs and a decrease in the supply of caregivers—have resulted in conversations about how policies might be able to address the situation, said Ibarrarán. Many people are currently not receiving the care they need; around 20% of older people report that they need help to perform basic activities of daily living but are not receiving care. The situation is not a "viable equilibrium," he said. These challenges

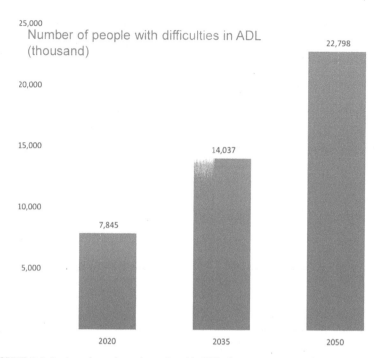

FIGURE 5-1 Projected number of people with difficulties in activities of daily living (ADL) in Latin America and the Caribbean.
SOURCE: Workshop presentation by Pablo Ibarrarán. Adapted from data in Aranco et al. (2022).

can only be overcome if the data needed to understand the specific needs and characteristics of countries and regions are available to design policies based on these needs. There is huge variation both within and across countries in terms of the supply and demand for care.

Unfortunately, current data sources are "very scarce and very heterogeneous," said Ibarrarán. There are two main data sources in the region that are relevant to aging and caregiving: surveys on health and aging and time-use surveys. Health and aging surveys include information about level of dependence, care arrangements, and basic caregiver characteristics. However, the data about caregivers are sparse, with no information about training or experience. The time-use surveys provide information about time spent by individuals in paid and unpaid work, time spent caring for others, and caregiver characteristics. Other data sources in the region include disability surveys, household surveys, and a recent Generations and Gender Survey in Uruguay[1] that looks at cultural changes regarding family and gender representations.

---

[1] https://ggp.colectica.org/item/int.ggp/e173d029-c667-43cc-8f51-83f8d3897c59/

While these surveys and studies are an excellent source of some data, policy making requires "much more precise information," said Ibarrarán. One challenge is a lack of consistency to enable comparison across countries. Data on labor force participation and poverty tend to be fairly consistent, but there is a lot of variation on measures of functional dependency. There are differences in the populations considered, the number and type of activities considered, the type and range of possible answers, and the wording used. There is a need to standardize and harmonize these tools so that the data can be compared within and across countries. Moreover, there are few countries that conduct multiple rounds of data collection. Mexico is an exception to this rule; the Estudio Nacional de Salud y Envejecimiento en México—National Survey of Health and Nutrition, in English—is an excellent source of quality data. Ibarrarán said that while surveys like this require a "considerable investment," it is a sound investment given their potential to inform policy making.

Ibarrarán described the efforts of IDB to increase knowledge about paid and unpaid caregivers in Latin America. Currently, little is known about paid caregivers because many care arrangements tend to be informal, with untrained caregivers. There are some countries, such as Costa Rica, with more developed formal caregiving markets. However, most caregiving in the region is provided by women in their mid-40s or 50s with low levels of education; only about one-third pay social security contributions. Labor force surveys provide some information in this area, but there are issues of capturing different types of care work and categorization (e.g., caregivers may be mixed in with those who do household work). IDB is trying to fill these gaps by carrying out a regional survey on around 330 unpaid caregivers and 550 paid caregivers who work in both homes and institutions. Six countries are participating. There are plans to extend to other countries and to conduct a longitudinal survey of paid care workers in the home setting.

Ibarrarán closed by stating that "We need to understand more so we can promote better policies." He offered several questions that are priority areas for future research:

- How has the gender division of care responsibilities evolved?
- How do care strategies affect the quality of life of dependent persons?
- How do care strategies affect the quality of life of family caregivers?
- What are the working conditions of paid care workers and how do they affect their quality of life and the care provided?

"I am convinced that the region can have a much better future for older persons," said Ibarrarán. There is an increasing awareness in governments of the importance of a society in which older people and their families have a good quality of life, with access to strong social protection networks that include long-term care services for all of those who need it. To reach this goal, one of the first steps is to gain a better understanding of the current conditions and to invest in data in order to evaluate and demonstrate the most efficient and most advantageous policies that can be implemented.

INTERGENERATIONAL TIES IN CHINA

China is similar to the rest of the world in that the population is aging, said Feinian Chen (Johns Hopkins University). However, the rate at which the population of older adults is rising is quite high in comparison with other nations: see Figure 5-2. China has a huge population, second only to India, so the 30% of the population that will be over 65 by the year 2050 translates to 360 million people. This rapid acceleration of the older population is "no surprise," said Chen, given the combination of the decrease in fertility and the increase in life expectancy in recent decades in the country.

Another major trend in China is a decline in family size and changes in family structure, said Chen. In 2020, the average family household was 2.61 individuals, compared with a high of 4.43 in 1964: see Figure 5-3. The decrease of household size coincides with a significant rise in one-generation households, although two- and multiple-generation households remain the most prevalent living arrangement among Chinese older adults as of 2018: see Figure 5-4. There has been massive internal migration in China over the last several decades, resulting in an increasing number of "skipped-generation households": households in which working-age adults leave their parents and children behind.

In China, "filial piety is considered the cornerstone of the old-age family support system," said Chen. The question, she said, is whether these recent trends in longevity, family size, and family structure will have a negative impact on family support and older adults' health and well-being. Chen shared her own research journey on the topic of living arrangements and intergenerational ties, which spanned from 2001 to 2023. The data for her research have come from four main sources: the China Health and Nutrition Survey, the Chinese Longitudinal Healthy Longevity Study, the China Health and Retirement Longitudinal Survey, and the China Longitudinal Aging Social Survey.

Evidence from these sources on the impact of living arrangements on health is mixed, said Chen. For example, a 2008 study found that living in a traditional extended household promotes subjective well-being. Results actually demonstrated that living with a daughter instead of a son improved well-being, in contradiction of the culturally preferred arrangement. In contrast, however, a 2018 study found that living in a multigenerational household offered limited health benefits to rural older adults, as measured

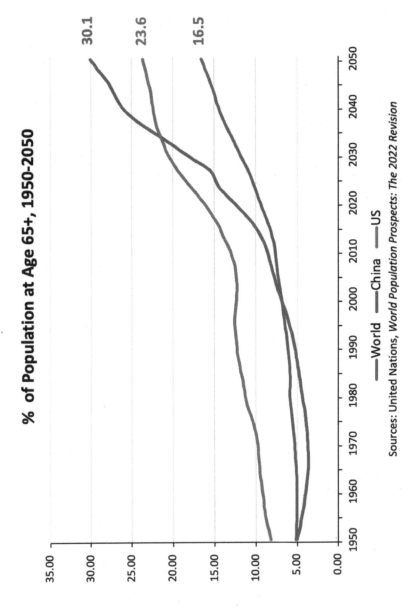

FIGURE 5-2 Trends in population aging for China, the United States, and the world.
SOURCE: Workshop presentation by Feinian Chen.

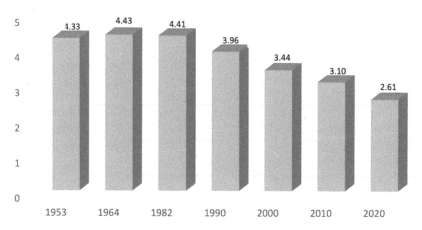

FIGURE 5-3 Average size of family households in China, 1953–2020.
SOURCE: Workshop presentation by Feinian Chen based on data from Chinese census.

FIGURE 5-4 Living arrangements for men and women aged 65+ in China, 2018.
SOURCE: Workshop presentation by Feinian Chen based on data from China Health and
Retirement Longitudinal Study, 2018.

by biomarkers. Chen said that these inconsistent findings demonstrated two challenges of studying living arrangements. First, a person's living arrangement is not random: a family's choice of living arrangement depends on societal norms, expectations, needs, and temperament. Second, it is important to look beyond living arrangements to consider the household composition of all of a person's living children. In addition, there are important family and friendship ties that go beyond the household. For example, a 2022 study found that friendship ties were associated with reduced depressive symptoms in older adults who lived alone (but not in older adults in other living arrangements), and nonhousehold family ties had the most positive effects on older adults living with children.

Chen and her colleagues have also examined living alone, loneliness, and social isolation as three forms of social disconnectedness. They found that just living alone is not a risk factor for poor life satisfaction. However, when living alone is combined with loneliness, it is clearly detrimental. Older adults who experience all three forms of social disconnectedness—living alone, loneliness, and social isolation—have the lowest life satisfaction of any group.

While living arrangements are clearly an important factor in older adults' health and well-being, there are other variables at play that should be studied. For example, for people who do not live with their children, proximity to children may matter, and the quality of the relationship with their children may matter. Chen and her colleagues found that life satisfaction was similar among adults who lived with children and had a high-quality relationship to those whose children lived close by and had a high-quality relationship. While older adults are often thought of as those who need care, they also provide care, said Chen. In China, in particular, grandparents play an important role in caregiving. Examining this role and its impact on health is another critical piece of the picture.

Chen shared a few lessons learned from China that may have implications for other LMICs. First, intergenerational ties have become ever more important in the 21st century. The extended household is still very important in China and many other countries, although some of the dynamics have shifted over time. Second, families are becoming more diverse and complicated globally. Demographers tend to look at families as units or households, but it is increasingly important to look at families as sets of relationships. Third, family obligations continue to exist, but the caring capacity of the family cannot be assumed, given trends in family size and the labor force. Finally, Chen emphasized the importance of "social embeddedness," which encompasses friendship ties, family ties, and social environment. Policies need to consider these ties beyond the household in order to maintain a strong support system for a rapidly aging society. In closing, Chen offered her "wish list" for new directions for research:

- grandparent–grandchild relationship as an important source of older-age support;
- parent–child dyadic analysis to further explore the linked lives;
- time-use diary data to capture detailed activities of older adults;
- data collection that starts before mid- and later-life; and
- leveraging existing longitudinal data other than aging surveys.

FAMILY TRENDS IN MEXICO

Family structure and the concept of family have changed dramatically recently, said Carmen García Peña (Instituto Nacional de Geriatria, Mexico). Family households are more fluid, with frequent changes in size and composition, and the fertility rate has dropped worldwide, particularly in Latin America. The average household size has declined, and there has been a sharp increase in the proportion of women in the labor force. Interestingly, the proportion of multigeneration households has increased in many Latin American countries since 2000; García-Peña suggested this is related to the problems faced during times of economic downturns. People are living longer, she said, but these extra years are not necessarily healthy. The difference between life expectancy and healthy life expectancy is around 8 to 10 years in most Latin American countries.

Aging in Mexico has been "accelerated and heterogeneous," said García-Peña. The proportion of older adults has risen rapidly, but the percentage of older adults in different regions of the country varies quite a bit. As in other Latin American countries, longevity has risen but there is still a difference of around 10 years between health-adjusted life expectancy at the age of 60 and life expectancy. This 10 years, she said, represents people living with functional dependency and the consequences of diseases, such as diabetes. Around 12% of adults over 60 live alone in Mexico, but around 70% of older people with severe functional dependency live alone. García-Peña said this is an "important challenge" to address. Another major challenge is the link between loneliness, social isolation, and mortality. A study in Mexico found results similar to those that Chen presented on China: social isolation increased the probability of dying after a fall by 1.3 times. Researchers concluded that a decrease in social interaction can affect the search for appropriate medical treatment, contribute to nonadherence to medications, and lead to unhealthy behaviors.

For better or worse, said García-Peña, the family is a crucial social determinant of health. Extended households can be a strategy for survival and interchange of supplies, but living with family can also be related to distress and abuse. Changes in family structure—from smaller family sizes to more flexible family structures—may have positive or negative effects on the well-being of older persons. There is a need for more research on how family relationships intersect with socioeconomic status and other factors to affect health and well-being, said García-Peña.

DISCUSSION

Minki Chatterji (National Institute on Aging) asked panelists about the status of social protection policies in Latin America, suggesting that it could be beneficial to prioritize research toward a country that is starting to do work in this area. Ibarrarán replied that there is a very wide range in terms of countries' social protection and care policies. Many countries have services for older people, but the services are not necessarily part of a broader policy implementation. Researchers are looking to evaluate small, specific interventions in order to build evidence about what works.

Will Dow (University of California, Berkeley) said that there is a need for more harmonized, longitudinal data in the Latin America region. It has been challenging, he said, to get regional budgetary buy-in for survey work. It could be useful to partner with others, such as the IDB and Pan American Health Organization, in order to advance this work. Ibarrarán said that partner organizations are beneficial for getting the process started and making recommendations, but that it is ideal if countries assume the ongoing costs of survey work. Emily Agree (John Hopkins University; workshop planning committee member) concurred and said it is easier for NIA to support harmonization than to fully fund a study; she encouraged participants to think about how partnerships could be initiated in high-value contexts. She added that there are existing data that are underutilized, for example, data on family structure in the MHAS. There could be an opportunity, she said, for NIA to incentivize the use of this rich source of data.

Chen noted that LMICs in all parts of the world are going through "very dramatic changes" in terms of demographics, family trends, policies, and socioeconomics. It is important to conduct research in order to tease apart the various changes and outcomes by taking many factors into consideration, including birth cohort and patterns across the life course.

6

Use of Existing Data

Key Points Highlighted by the Presenters:

• Longitudinal data are essential for studying aging; panel surveys that follow cohorts over time could be modified in order to include the collection of data relevant to aging. (**PALACIOS-LÓPEZ**)

• Existing sources of data relevant to aging have a number of disadvantages, but there are opportunities to leverage and improve these sources; new data privacy laws present some challenges to data use and sharing. (**NGUGI**)

• Using longitudinal and cohort studies can ensure that information about early-life experiences is accurate; it can be difficult for older adults to recall details later in life. (**STEPTOE**)

There is a great deal of existing data that could be leveraged to improve our knowledge of aging in low- and middle-income countries (LMICs), said David Weir (University of Michigan, planning committee member), who moderated the fifth session of the workshop. This session focused on identifying data in LMICs that may be of interest for examining life-course trajectories of development and aging, including early-life prospective data or retrospective data from current older cohorts; data linkages; or leveraging existing cohort studies established for other nonaging purposes. Presenters had been given a series of questions to guide their comments:

- What administrative linkages should we consider to enhance the utility of existing data?
- How can we continue to foster data sharing and deal with data sharing issues?
- What existing cohort studies might be used as samples for longitudinal studies of aging?
- What sampling frames (including administrative data, as well as censuses, etc.) are available to lower the cost of finding potential participants?

LONGITUDINAL HOUSEHOLD SURVEYS

The Living Standard Measurement Study (LSMS) is the World Bank's flagship household survey program, said Amparo Palacios-López (World Bank), virtual participant. It was created in 1980 in response to a perceived need for policy-relevant data for measuring poverty; it has since incorporated measures on employment, health, and other indicators. The objective, she said, is to allow policy makers to understand the determinants of these outcomes. The LSMS program has two components: one is focused on measuring living standards and the other is focused on studying the measurements themselves. LSMS supports countries in understanding the living standards of their populations by offering technical assistance and advisory services on all stages of the survey life cycle and by creating capacity within research institutes in client countries. LSMS engages in the study of measurement by conducting research on survey methods and by producing guidelines on best practices.[1]

Palacios-López explained that there are three ways that LSMS works with client countries: LSMS-led, LSMS-advised, and LSMS-style. An LSMS-led process is one in which LSMS is equal partners with the country and works to design and implement national-level methods under specific LSMS initiatives. In an LSMS-advised process, the LSMS team provides various levels of technical assistance to countries, such as help with revising a questionnaire. An LSMS-style process is one in which a country uses free LSMS materials with no team involvement. Countries use the guidelines that LSMS has produced and implement their own living standards, said Palacios-López.

The main focus of LSMS has been LMICs, said Palacios-López, with a particular focus on Africa. One specific effort in African countries is the Living Standards Measurement Study—Integrated Surveys on Agriculture (LSMS-ISA).[2] This is a unique system of longitudinal surveys designed to

---

[1] https://www.worldbank.org/en/programs/lsms/overview
[2] https://www.worldbank.org/en/programs/lsms/initiatives/lsms-ISA

improve the understanding of household and individual welfare, livelihoods, and smallholder agriculture in Africa. The program has been in op-
eration for more than 15 years, and it has focused on three different work
streams. The first stream is data production. LSMS supports the design,
implementation, and dissemination of country-owned, multitopic, national
panel household surveys. The main difference between these and other similar surveys, said Palacios-López, is that they are panel household surveys;
there are datasets of households or individuals that are followed over time.

The second work stream of LSMS-ISA is focused on methods and tools.
In this effort, LSMS and partner countries work to improve methods and
tools for survey data collection and analysis through field experiments and
rigorous research and development. Palacios-López shared an example of
a methodological experiment conducted in Malawi aimed at finding ways
to measure time use. Researchers gave participants smart phones to record
activities over the course of the day; many participants could not read or
write but were able to use images to create a time-use recording. The third
work stream of LSMS-ISA is conducting and promoting research to inform
evidence-based development policies.

LSMS has been working with national statistical offices in eight partner
countries: Burkina Faso, Ethiopia, Malawi, Mali, Niger, Nigeria, Tanzania,
and Uganda. Together, these countries make up 45% of the population of
sub-Saharan Africa, Palacios-López noted. The surveys are integrated into
the national statistical systems and implemented by the national statistical
offices. They track households and individuals and are representative at the
national and regional levels. The surveys use a specific agricultural model
designed to collect as much information as possible to inform agricultural
policy. Surveys are georeferenced at the household level and the plot level.
Computer-assisted personal and telephone interviewing are used to conduct
the survey, and all of the data are publicly available.

Palacios-López shared some numbers on the impact of LSMS-ISA:

- 33 surveys,
- 160,000+ household interviews,
- 81,000+ dataset downloads,
- 6,400+ total publications,
- 3,000+ total citations,
- 20+ guidebooks, and
- 1400+ guidebook downloads.

More specifically, Palacios-López discussed some selected data from
the LSMS surveys. Using surveys from Nigeria and Tanzania, she said she
used harmonized longitudinal data and selected the 4 oldest cohorts. She
noted that while the data are representative of the country's population in

general, they may not be representative of the older population specifically. In addition, the surveys do not contain indicators specific to aging or older populations, but there are many indicators that may be relevant. She looked at data on employment status, type of work, health care access, and functional limitations. As expected, employment wanes over time as individuals age, but they still are quite active. In Nigeria, the majority of people 40 and older are employed; of those who are employed, the oldest age group (70+) had the largest share of individuals working in agriculture. Palacios-López noted that while agriculture is a physically demanding job, it is also one that provides subsistence, so it may be used as "insurance" when things do not go well in other sectors. Survey questions about health care found that needs for and access to health care providers rose along with respondents' ages. In addition, the oldest cohort showed a much higher share of individuals reporting functional limitations.

Longitudinal studies are critical for studying different indicators over time, said Palacios-López. They can provide information on the evolution of different cohorts and support the design of policies that target the aging population. LSMS panel data are a good example of this type of survey, with rich information on sociodemographics. If the LSMS were to be used for aging-specific research, it would be useful to ensure that the sample is representative of older populations and to add modules that are relevant to aging populations in LMICs.

DATA LANDSCAPE IN KENYA

The African population is aging very rapidly, said Anthony Ngugi (The Aga Khan University). In 2020, less than 6% of the population was older than 60. By 2050, this number is projected to increase to around 15%, with the number even higher in some nations. At the same time as this demographic transition is occurring, there is an equally rapid epidemiologic transition with an increase in chronic disease and disability. These transitions are happening, he said, in an area in which there are scarce population-level data on critical domains of aging, such as health, mental health, climate vulnerability, and economic well-being. Data are needed to inform responses to the unique health and socioeconomic challenges that will emerge as the population ages.

There are several likely sources of data that could be explored for evidence related to aging. These include Health Management Information Systems (HMISs); national or regional surveys (e.g., health surveys); longitudinal population studies; and health and demographic surveillance systems (HDSSs), including the use of bureaus of statistics' sampling frames for additional population data collection. Ngugi discussed each of these in turn, using Kenya as an example.

The HMIS collects data for a specific service or demographic in a facility-based register, and at the end of the month data are aggregated for submission to a higher HMIS office (e.g., subnational level). From each of these offices, data are aggregated again to be transmitted to the national HMIS. Ngugi emphasized that most individual-level data are left at the health facility, usually in paper forms, and only aggregate data are transmitted upward. There is no register for capturing information from the geriatric population since no specific service is designated for this group, said Ngugi. "With really intense effort" it may be possible to extract data on older populations from other registers, such as from inpatient or outpatient registers (for people over 5 years old). In addition to this limitation, HMIS suffers from poor availability of data, poor data quality, and low capacity for processing and use of data for decision making. A study on the collection of maternal child health data found that only about 6% of counties had good reporting of deliveries, and only about 26% had good reporting of outpatient visits. Overall, said Ngugi, data quality is low, with incomplete and inconsistent information. HMIS data present "really serious challenges" to its potential utility for informing studies of health and aging, he said.

National or regional surveys are another potential source of data for studies on aging. For example, Kenya conducts the National Population & Housing Census Surveys every 10 years: it collects information on the population classified by geographical units, age, sex, socioeconomic status (SES), and other parameters. One of the most important outputs of the census, he said, is that it informs the generation of nationally representative sampling frames. The last census in Kenya led to the generation of close to 6,000 sampling clusters of about 100 households each across the country. This enabled the nationally representative surveys to be developed, including demographic and health surveys. These surveys collect household information about housing, SES, HIV, chronic disease, and other measures. Thus, the census might be a place to implement nationally representative surveys of aging, said Ngugi. Another promising source of data is the registry of beneficiaries for the National Safety Net Program. This social protection program began 3 years ago and targets vulnerable children and adults over 70, with plans to reduce the eligibility age to 65. Recipients are identified and registered through an intensive grassroots effort, and their information is held at the Department of Social Protection. This registry, said Ngugi, could be a source for identifying potential participants for aging studies.

Longitudinal population studies have an important place in aging research, although there are currently only two in Kenya specifically on aging: the Health and Aging in Africa: A Longitudinal Study in South Africa (HAALSI) and the Longitudinal Study of Health and Aging in Kenya

(LOSHAK).[3] Ngugi noted that other longitudinal studies in Kenya are disease- or condition-specific—for example, the Network for Analysing Longitudinal Population-based HIV/AIDS data on Africa,[4] and the H3Africa Consortium[5] on genomics.

HDSSs are platforms that continuously track the demographics and health of large, well-defined cohorts. These exist in several LMICs in Africa and Asia and provide robust infrastructure resources for nesting longitudinal population studies, said Ngugi. One of the challenges of HDSSs, however, is that they are not nationally representative. In addition, the characteristics of participating populations can change over time toward improved health outcomes; this change gradually makes the sample less similar to the broader population.

Given the drawbacks of these sources of data for studying aging, said Ngugi, he asked whether there is potential for linking data across the various sources. Unfortunately, he said, there is "limited feasibility" of linking due primarily to the limited potential for harmonizing. There are no unique identifiers used across databases, as most sources are designed by different stakeholders. Moreover, as he said earlier, the data in many sources, particularly HMISs, are of poor quality in terms of availability, completeness, timeliness, and consistency. Using statistical methods to link data sources is challenging due to nonstandard respondent identification information across surveys, even in the same population (e.g., name, dates of birth, locality).

Despite these challenges, said Ngugi, there are many stakeholders working on data in Africa who recognize these problems and are taking active steps to address them. One initiative is the African Population Cohort Consortium, funded by the Wellcome Trust. It is designed to bring together longitudinal population studies that track the health of large groups of people and to develop resources where gaps exist. When this project is mature, it will provide a pan-African network that can be used to host longitudinal population studies in the region.

Another promising project is the Implementation Network for Sharing Population Information from Research Entities (INSPIRE Network);[6] this project is focused on data harmonization and works to empower data producers to collect data that are sharable. In addition, the INSPIRE Network works with data users and provides tools for data discoverability. Researchers and other stakeholders who have an interest in longitudinal studies of health and aging should consider engaging with these initiatives,

---

[3] https://sites.google.com/umich.edu/loshak/home and https://academic.oup.com/innovateage/article/7/Supplement_1/1155/7490267

[4] https://academic.oup.com/ije/article/45/1/83/2363877

[5] https://h3africa.org/

[6] https://aphrc.org/project/inspire-implementation-network-for-sharing-population-information-from-research-entities/

said Ngugi. Also, there is tremendous potential to leverage existing data platforms in order to further research on aging. For example, the National Sample Survey and Evaluation Programme that is generated out of each census has been utilized for national surveys on conditions such as AIDS or malaria; researchers on aging could do likewise. LOSHAK is using the census frames to identify participants for national data collection, collaborating with the Kenya National Bureau of Statistics on this effort. In addition, researchers can explore the potential to piggyback on national surveys that are conducted on a regular basis by adding modules on aging.

Ngugi closed by identifying some of the data sharing considerations and challenges in Africa. The data governance landscape has shifted dramatically over the last several years, particularly since the passage of data protection regulations in Europe in 2016. The number of countries in Africa with comprehensive data protection laws has more than doubled, from about 15 to more than 30. Kenya enacted the Kenya Data Protection Act in 2019; this act made a number of important changes:

- enhanced the constitutional provisions on right to privacy;
- established the Office of the Data Protection Commissioner;
- regulated the processing of personal data;
- provided for the rights of data "subjects" and obligations of data "controllers" and "processors"; and
- outlined stiff penalties for noncompliance.

Many institutions in Kenya are currently establishing frameworks to ensure compliance, said Ngugi. Although new data collection initiatives need to complete elaborate Data Protection & Privacy Impact Assessments (DPPIAs), research data appear to be exempt from most provisions if they meet certain standards, including specific and adequate consent from subjects, data are sufficiently anonymized, personal data are not transferred outside the country, and a DPPIA is completed and submitted. These new regulations are restrictive, said Ngugi, but not prohibitive. It is critical for all stakeholders, including international partners, to work with local stakeholders to navigate these data governance regulations.

KEY CHALLENGES IN DATA

Andrew Steptoe (University College London) discussed the key data challenges and opportunities that other presenters identified, focusing on 3 questions:

1. How can we use existing cohort studies of younger people in LMICs for aging research?
2. How robust are retrospective assessments of early- and midlife experience?
3. What are the challenges of administrative data linkage and sharing?

There are a number of existing cohort studies that could be leveraged to study aging in LMICs, said Steptoe. The Health and Retirement Study (HRS) International Family of Studies began in higher-income countries, but there has been growing involvement of lower-income countries, including Mexico, Brazil, South Africa, China, and Kenya. Studies that focus on younger cohorts may not be immediately relevant to aging research but could be important in the future as cohorts age. These are often not nationally representative but tend to be quite representative in terms of SES. These studies include the Pelotas Birth Cohort study in Brazil, the Cebu Longitudinal Health and Nutrition Study in the Philippines, the Guatemalan Survey of Family Health, and the New Delhi Birth Cohort Study, among others. In addition, the World Bank Living Standard Measurement Study Program, as discussed by Palacios-López, has impressive data on demographics, standards of living, and work across aged cohorts.

Steptoe noted several challenges with repurposing general studies for aging research. First, attrition can be high in longitudinal studies, particularly as people age. Second, studies that were designed for one purpose (e.g., child health) may lack the measures needed to study aging—for example, health behaviors, cognitive changes, or loneliness. Third, it is critical to obtain consent from participants for further contact once the initial study is completed. Failing to do this can cause challenges, and newer data privacy laws have made it very difficult to reestablish contact with participants.

Next, Steptoe discussed the robustness of retrospective assessments of early- and midlife experiences. This is a crucial issue for aging studies, he said, because they often depend on this kind of information. Factors such as early-life SES, adverse childhood experiences, reproductive history, occupational history, and health behaviors in midlife are typically assessed with retrospective life history questionnaires; examples include Survey of Health, Ageing and Retirement in Europe (SHARES), Health and Retirement Study (HRS), China Health and Retirement Longitudinal Study (CHARLS), and English Longitudinal Study of Ageing (ELSA). Life history questionnaires need to be presented with care, said Steptoe, because it can be difficult for some older people to recall the exact timing of different experiences earlier in their lives. Some experiences are easier to recall than others. Marital history, number of children, and occupations are likely to be accurate, but things like body weight or physical activity patterns are very difficult for people to recall retrospectively. There have been several efforts to compare concurrent and retrospective accounts. One such effort found that children whose parents reported at the time that they experienced chronic health conditions and financial hardship did not always remember these realities when asked for a retrospective account later in life. Steptoe said that this is not surprising, given that children may not be particularly aware of their health challenges or their family's financial problems, but it does highlight a need for caution in looking at these types of data (Smith, 2009).

Finally, Steptoe touched on the challenges of administrative data linking and sharing. Administrative data provide a great source of information, including records from social security, Medicare-type programs, employee-provided pension plan information, national death records, hospital admissions, and outpatient consultations. Linking to these sources is going to vary greatly across countries, he said, and in the United Kingdom and Europe linkage is getting more restricted. Data privacy laws have made stakeholders "very nervous" about sharing with researchers in other countries, making the development of widely available data linkage a serious challenge. This is a critical issue, he said, that needs to be resolved in many countries, and it needs to be resolved at a higher level rather than on a case-by-case basis.

DISCUSSION

The speakers in this session, said Minki Chatterji (National Institute on Aging), presented a number of opportunities for leveraging existing data and also a number of challenges associated with using these data. Some of these opportunities seem like "low-hanging fruit," but she emphasized the importance of focusing on the most important research questions to answer and working backward toward the data. It can be easy to get "mired" in all the data, but data are not helpful if they are not aligned with the priorities of the research agenda. For example, she said, existing cohort studies present an enormous opportunity for aging research, but it is critical to think about the questions in order to pinpoint the data that are relevant and important. Another major opportunity is triangulating sets of data in order to answer research questions. However, she noted, data sharing remains a big challenge that needs to be addressed.

Ngugi agreed that data sharing is a big challenge, but he said that there are solutions that can move research forward. For example, he and his colleagues are using data science approaches that allow researchers to analyze datasets without holding or viewing the data themselves (e.g., federated analyses, or generating synthetic datasets out of the original data). These solutions are not "100%," he said, but they may be useful in a context in which data sharing is difficult or impossible.

Mary Ganguli (University of Pittsburgh; workshop planning committee member) noted two concerns with data sharing that need to be addressed. First, there are ways that deidentified data can be reidentified, so it is important to understand and address this concern. Second, some of the disclosures required by data privacy laws—such as telling participants about using their data in national repositories or for commercial application—are difficult to explain to any research participant, but particularly those in LMICs. Ngugi replied that there has always been a concern about researchers using data from people in LMICs and "making their careers out of it." Some of the hesitations about data sharing, he said, stem from this concern: communities who spend time and resources collecting data want to be able to analyze and control their own data. This is one reason why building research capacity in LMICs is critically important, he said.

Ngugi shared one approach for analyzing data that stay in the hands of others. Ghana has made 10% of the data from their household census available; researchers can develop an analytical code and test it in the 10%. If it works, the researcher works with Ghana to run the code on the entire dataset and extract indicators, but the physical data stay with Ghana. Chatterji added that another approach is using a data enclave; given all of the concerns about data sharing, this could be a high-priority area for investments.

Ganguli asked Palacios-López whether the World Bank would be open to broadening the focus of their living standard measurement surveys to include indicators of health. This could be done in 3 ways, said Weir: (1) add a health component to the survey, (2) select some participants for a follow-on study that focuses on health, or (3) allow a third-party group to follow up with participants to conduct a health study. Palacios-López replied that the first option—adding a health component to the survey—would be the most palatable to the World Bank because the organization follows households over a long period of time and would not want to "hand off" participants to another party. The surveys actually have included health and nutrition indicators, and the World Bank is working to modify the surveys in the future to put a larger focus on health and climate change.

7

Role of Environmental Exposures

Key Points Highlighted by the Presenters

- Household air pollution is a major contributor to poor health in low- and middle-income countries (LMICs) and a contributor to climate change globally; more research is needed to understand how to develop the most effective interventions to address this problem. (**ADAR**)

- Events related to climate change can have dramatic affects on the health, well-being, and economic situation of affected populations, but these affects vary considerably; studies that track populations before and after an event are necessary in order to learn more about what factors contribute to variation in health and well-being. (**FRANKENBERG**)

- The affect of environmental hazards and climate change on the health and well-being of older adults depends on complex interactions between exposure and vulnerability, as well as potential for resilience and adaptation; LMICs lack some key resources that higher-income countries have to confront environmental challenges, but they may be more innovative and motivated to adapt to changing environmental conditions. (**AILSHIRE**)

Mary Ganguli (University of Pittsburgh; planning committee member), who chaired the session, noted that low- and middle-income countries (LMICs) are the most vulnerable to the effects of climate change and other environmental exposures. Given this, the sixth session of the workshop focused on how environmental exposures affect the health and well-being of older populations in LMICs. Several questions guided the presentations and discussion:

- What are the mechanisms through which exposures operate?
- What adaptation and mitigation strategies have been or need to be developed to reduce the harmful effects of environmental exposure?
- To what extent are the impacts of exposure on health outcomes specific to LMICs, given their country-specific contexts?

HOUSEHOLD AIR POLLUTION AND HEALTH IN LMICS

Humans have almost always used fire as a way to cook their food, and for heating, light, and protection, said Sara Adar (University of Michigan). In high-income settings, most people use fairly clean fuel for cooking and heating. In low-income settings, however, 3 billion people are burning solid fuels for cooking and heating, such as wood, animal waste, and coal. Burning these substances is inefficient and releases numerous pollutants into the air, including carbon monoxide, fine particulate matter ($PM_{2.5}$), polycyclic aromatic hydrocarbons (PAHs), formaldehyde, benzene, volatile organic carbons, nitrogen dioxide, and sulfur dioxide.

A wood-fired three-stone stove, said Adar, produces the same amount of smoke in 1 hour as 400 cigarettes and, in 1 year, the same amount as 20 diesel trucks each driving 30,000 miles. People cooking over a fire are generally very close to the fire, and they are exposed to 10–100 times a healthy level of smoke. In addition to irritating a person's eyes and throat, smoke exposures have long-term health implications, including inflammation of the lungs and systemic inflammation that can affect the rest of the body. The smallest particles can get into the bloodstream and may even travel into the brain through the nose. Adar presented data on the relative risk of various outcomes that are associated with the use of burning fuels, including lung cancer, cardiovascular diseases, adverse pregnancy outcomes, and asthma: see Figure 7-1. Burning of polluting fuels has also been associated with a higher risk of mortality, including under-5 mortality, cardiovascular mortality, respiratory mortality, and all-cause mortality.

Researchers have estimated that the global burden of disease due to the household burning of polluting fuels is approximately 1.8 million premature deaths and 60.9 million disability-adjusted life years lost (Lee et al., 2020). These burdens are almost entirely carried by LMICs, said Adar.

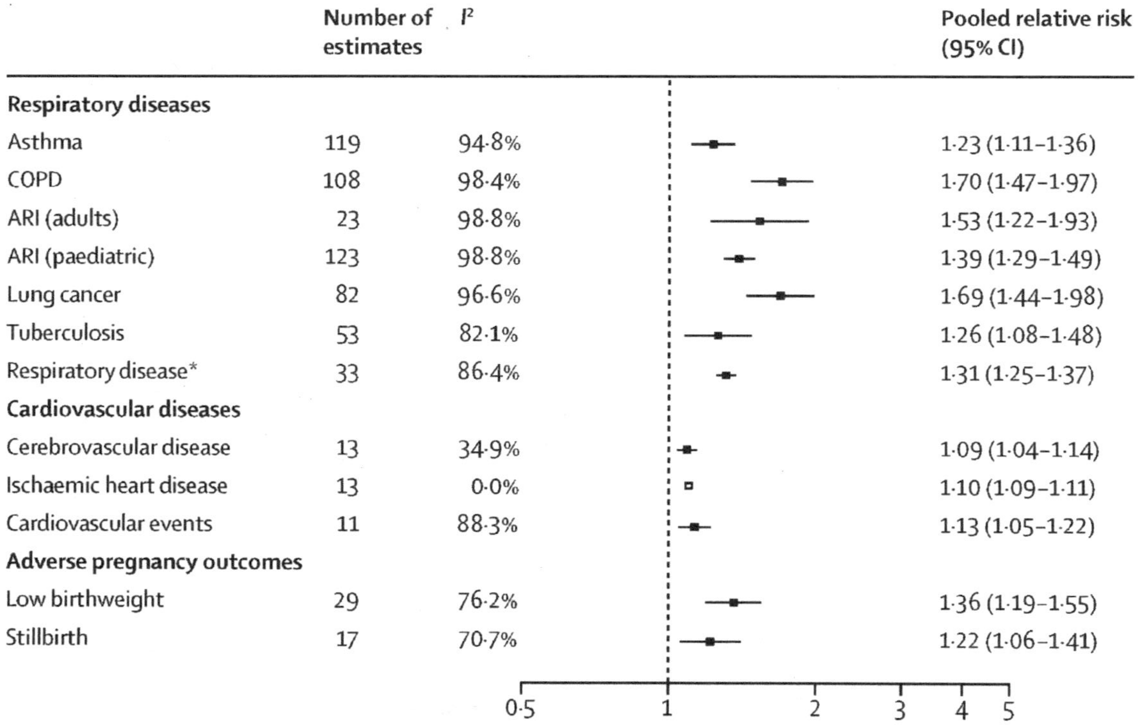

	Number of estimates	I^2		Pooled relative risk (95% CI)
Respiratory diseases				
Asthma	119	94·8%		1·23 (1·11–1·36)
COPD	108	98·4%		1·70 (1·47–1·97)
ARI (adults)	23	98·8%		1·53 (1·22–1·93)
ARI (paediatric)	123	98·8%		1·39 (1·29–1·49)
Lung cancer	82	96·6%		1·69 (1·44–1·98)
Tuberculosis	53	82·1%		1·26 (1·08–1·48)
Respiratory disease*	33	86·4%		1·31 (1·25–1·37)
Cardiovascular diseases				
Cerebrovascular disease	13	34·9%		1·09 (1·04–1·14)
Ischaemic heart disease	13	0·0%		1·10 (1·09–1·11)
Cardiovascular events	11	88·3%		1·13 (1·05–1·22)
Adverse pregnancy outcomes				
Low birthweight	29	76·2%		1·36 (1·19–1·55)
Stillbirth	17	70·7%		1·22 (1·06–1·41)

FIGURE 7-1 Pooled relative risks (across studies) for cardiovascular, respiratory, and adverse pregnancy outcomes associated with use of polluting fuels and technologies.

NOTE: ARI, acute respiratory infection; COPD, chronic obstructive pulmonary disease.

SOURCE: Lee et al. (2020, Figure 1). Reprinted under Creative Commons 4.0 license: https://creativecommons.org/licenses/by/4.0/

The largest burden is in Southeast Asia, Africa, and the western Pacific. Highly polluting household fuels are also associated with lower cognitive function. Using harmonized datasets, Adar said that she and her colleagues found that higher exposures to highly polluting fuels for household heating and cooking were associated with more cognitive deficits. The impact was significant, she said, with deficits equivalent to about 3–6 years (Saenz et al., 2021).

There have been many efforts by both governments and individual groups to try to reduce exposures by providing better cookstoves or cleaner sources of fuel. Better cookstoves burn cleaner or use chimneys to vent smoke outside of the home. The benefits of this type of intervention, said Adar, is that it reduces exposure while allowing people to use the fuel that they are accustomed to. The drawbacks are the costs of the equipment and the upkeep that it might require. The benefits of a chimney system are not as large as one might expect, since the smoke goes outside but can come back into the home through doors and windows. Another option for reducing exposure is providing cleaner fuel, such as liquified petroleum gas or ethanol. These substances are not "perfectly clean," but they are much better than the current fuels being used. The challenge with this type of intervention is the practical aspects of continued access, including refilling cylinders and ensuring a steady supply to remote communities. There can also be cultural challenges, said Adar, such as fears of cylinders exploding in their home. Adar noted that when given new sources of fuel, some people will actually use both the new fuel and the old fuel (e.g., wood). A third type of intervention is called "leapfrogging": moving people all the way to the cleanest types of cooking, such as induction or solar energy. The major drawbacks of this intervention are high cost and lack of available resources (e.g., constant supply of electricity).

Research has found that these interventions are effective in reducing exposures, both in personal exposure and the concentration of pollution in the kitchen. However, Adar noted that none of the interventions have succeeded in getting levels down to goals by the World Health Organization for "low concentrations" of pollution. Furthermore, the reductions in exposure have not always led to measurable improvements in health. Adar said that there are two potential reasons for this disconnect. First, while exposures are lower, they are still high enough to cause damage to the body. Second, interventions on individual homes may not be effective if other homes in the community continue to burn highly polluting fuel since this smoke can pass from home to home as it contaminates the outdoor air. It may be necessary, she said, to intervene in entire communities in order to have the significant effects on people's health.

The impact of interventions aimed at reducing the use of polluting fuels reach far beyond the targeted individuals and communities, said Adar. The burning of these fuels is causing deforestation, generating greenhouse gases, and generating short-lived pollutants in the air that absorb heat and keep it in the atmosphere. Helping people replace their cookstoves or fuel sources can improve their health and also affect people across the globe. In addition, she noted, climate change is increasing the number and intensity of wildfires; wildfire smoke is contributing greater portions of people's yearly exposures to air pollution, even in the United States. Adar said that there is also research from her research group to show that wildfire smoke may be one of the more toxic sources of particulate pollution for the brain (Zhang et al., 2023).

There are many future opportunities in this area for further research, said Adar, including:

- further examination of the effects of household air pollution;
- understanding "how low is low enough?";
- better exposure assessment;
- better consideration of the outcomes for aging and aging populations;
- implementation research;
- the impacts of and resilience to climate change;
- understand the heterogeneity of people's experiences; and
- capacity building and models that promote LMIC investigators.

HEALTH IMPACTS OF CLIMATE CHANGE IN LMICS

There are multiple components of climate change and climate shocks, said Elizabeth Frankenberg (University of North Carolina). The physical dimensions of climate change include exposure to wind, rainfall, and drought; humidity; temperature; sea level and tides; and ground saturation. Climate events vary across different parameters, including speed of onset, predictability, duration, scale, and chronic or acute. The impact of these events can be far-reaching and wide-ranging, and can include property damage, exposure to physical threats, changes in work opportunities, disruption of daily activities, disruption to social networks, reduced access to health care, and rising prices.

The degree to which people and communities are affected by climate change and climate shocks, said Frankenberg, varies depending on demographic, economic, and social factors. There is an increasing frequency and intensity of extreme events, she said, and these are occurring against a backdrop of changing baseline conditions. Biologists see this as a "pulse and press" framework, in which the "new normal" of more devastating fires, storms, and hurricanes occurs more often and lasts longer, and there is less recovery time between events. Social scientists need to consider such questions as:

- To what extent does an event affect health, increase mortality, or both?
- What are the impacts on livelihoods, assets, and socioeconomic well-being?
- What resources are available to support a postevent recovery phase?
- Does the biology of aging or the evolution of socioeconomic status that accompanies aging diminish people's ability to respond and adapt?

As people age, Frankenberg said, they may experience reduced physical mobility, greater frailty, cognitive decline, and diminished thermal regulation. They may also have fewer ways of coping with and mitigating the effects of climate change, including limited economic resources, shrinking social and family networks, anxiety about change, and a deep attachment to place.

Measurements and methods that are important in the context of assessing the impact of climate change include constructing accurate measurements of climate-related physical forces, collecting evidence from populations both before and after a climate event, and establishing dose–response relationships using a natural experiment framework.

To illustrate her points, Frankenberg talked about the 2004 Sumatra Andaman earthquake and tsunami that affected 26 countries, focusing specifically on Aceh, Indonesia. The earthquake occurred about 150 kilometers off the coast and involved a 1,200 kilometer "unzipping" of the sea floor. A series of tsunami waves were set off and hit Aceh about 15 minutes after the earthquake. The tsunami was unexpected (the last to hit Aceh was over 600 years ago), and there was local variation in impact that was driven by offshore topography. People had little to no time to move before the waves hit. About 200,000 people were killed—about 5% of the province's population—and about 750,000 were displaced. The "beautiful, idyllic coastal landscape" with fields, roads, and settlement was replaced by bare earth. There was a strong effort to raise money for recovery; assistance funds raised totaled $7 billion. Within 5 years after the tsunami, the area had made substantial strides toward recovery, with beaches, roads, homes, and fields beginning to return.

Frankenberg and her colleagues conducted the Study of the Tsunami Aftermath and Recovery (STAR),[1] which used as a baseline pre-tsunami

---

[1] http://stardata.org/

data from a government survey that had collected information on 26,000 individuals. Researchers followed up with 96% of survivors and followed people who had moved all over Indonesia. They conducted 5 years of annual surveys immediately after the tsunami, then moved to surveys every 5 years; these were interspersed with collections of more extensive biomarkers and cognitive data on a subsample of participants. Survey domains included household composition, economic resources, education, migration, work, fertility, psychosocial health, tsunami shocks, loneliness, sleep, frailty, memory, social support, and networks.

Frankenberg presented information on mortality among the residents of Aceh. Clearly, initial mortality rates were highest in the communities that were hardest hit by the tsunami. However, in the 10 years following the tsunami, the hardest-hit communities actually experienced lower mortality. She suggested that this reflected a positive selection effect: namely, that those who survived were selected on factors that promote longevity. There were particular "scarring" experiences related to the tsunami that affected the prospects of survival for adults 50 and older. For females, losing a spouse reduced survival. For males, losing a spouse increased survival, while living in temporary housing or experiencing high levels of post-traumatic stress reactivity decreased survival. There was no evidence of such "scarring" for younger adults, she said.

Exposure to the tsunami was found to affect cognitive and biological functioning, said Frankenberg. Males who lived in communities that were badly damaged had worse cognitive scores, as did females who saw or heard the water as a personal exposure. Two markers that are associated with stroke and cardiovascular disease (C-reactive protein and adiposity) were increased in both females and males who lived in communities that were heavily damaged; this effect was found 12 years after the tsunami (Frankenberg et al., 2018).

The economic impact of the tsunami was long lasting, said Frankenberg. For example, 10 years after the tsunami, the earnings of men who were aged 40 to 60 when they were directly exposed to the tsunami were 30% lower than before the tsunami, and 30% lower than the earnings of men who were not directly exposed. For directly exposed younger men, earnings recovered over time, but they remained 12% lower than those who were not directly exposed. There are a number of mechanisms driving these differences, said Frankenberg. A lot of earnings recovery was driven by reconstruction; these opportunities are more available to younger men. In response to the tsunami and its impact, women entered the labor market, households started businesses and took on financial risks, and families sold assets. Assistance was critical to survivors: 21% of survey respondents received an assistance home, and receipt was more likely among those with fewer resources before the disaster. Those who received a home showed a decline in post-traumatic stress reactivity levels, and this effect was concentrated among those whose homes were destroyed. Frankenberg said that this study demonstrated a critical nexus between housing and psychosocial health (Frankenberg et al., 2023).

In summary, Frankenberg said that exposure to the effects of climate change creates stressors that affect physical, psychosocial, and cognitive health over the short and longer term. The financial, social, and human resources with which people enter midlife are likely critical for how old age unfolds with respect to the effects of climate change for health and economics. She noted that "institutions matter" by reducing exposures and the consequences of exposure, and institutions vary hugely across LMICs. Frankenberg identified some key questions that remain for future research:

- What are cost-effective strategies for preventing or facilitating recovery from large negative climate shocks or less severe but more frequent events?
- What are the general equilibrium effects on economic and social systems?
- How do these dynamics intersect with the aging process to generate differential vulnerability?

Regarding research infrastructure, Frankenberg emphasized several lessons learned from the STAR study. First, tracking people both before and after an event is key; this may mean following people long term to other locations. Second, there is a need to conceptualize and measure exposure, to assess its exogeneity, and to capture variation in exposure. The dose–exposure relationship is important and can reveal interesting patterns. Third, national representation is not always the highest priority for studies of environmental exposures. Heterogeneity in exposure is important, as is having a large enough sample size to be able to drill down into finer-grained questions. Fourth, there are scientific opportunities in building networks of studies using a natural experiment "dose of exposure" framework. Comparisons across studies of different events and populations will be fruitful. Finally, adding and evaluating the impact of interventions is key to reducing consequences for the health and well-being of affected populations.

ENVIRONMENTAL RISKS AND ADAPTATIONS IN LMICS

Jennifer Ailshire (University of Southern California) provided a broad view of the topic of environmental risks and how they may affect the health of older populations in LMICs. She began by sharing a framework for environmental impacts on health in LMICs: see Figure 7-2. Risk is formed through the interaction of hazards, exposure, and vulnerability. Hazards

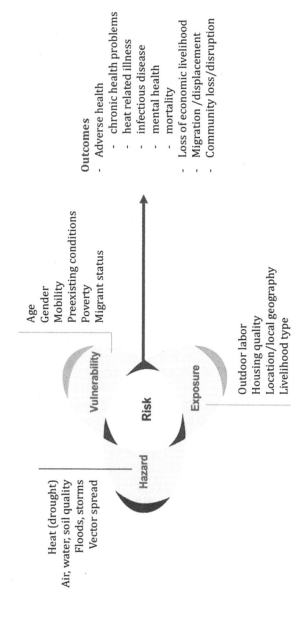

FIGURE 7-2 Framework for environmental impacts on health in low- and middle-income countries.
SOURCE: Adapted from Cissé et al. (2022, Figure 7.4).

can include heat, air and water quality, floods, storms, and the spread of vector-borne diseases. The potential for exposure is related to the context in which people live, and it can include such factors as housing quality, work environment, location, and type of work. Ailshire noted that people in LMICs are often more likely to be exposed to hazards due to their location and lifestyle. For example, people working outdoors are exposed to poor air quality, people living in substandard housing are less protected from storms, and people who work in agriculture may lose work opportunities because of drought or land damage. Hazard and exposure interact with an individual's vulnerability factors, which include age, gender, mobility, preexisting conditions, poverty, and migrant status.

There are a wide variety of ways that these factors can make a person more environmentally vulnerable, she said. For example, a lack of mobility can make it harder to move away from a fast-moving event (e.g., flood), women may be exposed to indoor air pollution from cooking, men may be exposed to poor air quality outdoors, poor people lack resources to mitigate or cope with climate events, and people with preexisting conditions may have exacerbated outcomes. Migrants may be particularly vulnerable, said Ailshire, because of such factors as informal work arrangements, poor-quality housing, and lack of eligibility for social support and health care services that might be provided to the rest of the population after an environmental event.

Taken together, hazards, exposure, and vulnerability create risks, which can translate into outcomes. Outcomes can be health related, such as chronic health problems, infectious disease, mortality, and mental health issues. Outcomes can also include loss of economic livelihood, forced migration or displacement, and the loss or disruption of community. Ailshire noted that people in LMICs who live, work, and socialize in the same small community may be more affected by a localized event than people in higher-income areas. For example, she noted that in high-income countries a fire that threatens a person's home is unlikely to also threaten their place of work since they tend to be located in different places; this is less so in low-income countries.

Ailshire shared three maps that show the predicted future impact of air pollution, extreme heat, and mosquito-borne illness across the globe. In each map, the biggest impacts are in countries in Latin America, Africa, and Asia. Compounding these projected risks, said Ailshire, is that many of these countries have rapidly growing older populations, developing economies that are shifting to more industrialization and more pollution, a lack of urban planning or standards for building, and inadequate health care systems. Furthermore, she said, these countries often lack the wealth at both the individual and macro levels to invest in technology to mitigate these risks (e.g., to buy air conditioners for rising heat). Older adults in these countries have specific challenges that make them more vulnerable, including:

- greater health burdens that exacerbate adverse environmental events;
- lack of access to health care;
- limited social protection programs targeted to them;
- changes in urbanization, economic development, and family configurations; and
- inadequate economic resources for recovery in event of environmental adversity.

The extent to which the hazard–exposure–vulnerability nexus translates into risk depends on a population's ability to be resilient or to develop adaptation strategies, said Ailshire. The Intergovernmental Panel on Climate Change offers a clear definition of resilience and adaptation: "Human vulnerability is influenced by the adaptive capacity of physical (built) structures, social processes (economic, well-being and health) and institutional structures (organisations, laws, cultural and political systems/ norms)" (Dodman et al., 2022, p. 929). Ailshire said that she likes this definition because it does not put the onus of resilience on individuals or families, but instead acknowledges that it will take macro-level changes and macro-level actors to facilitate resilience in communities. There are a number of ways that LMIC communities can become more resilient or adapt to changes, including:

- early warning systems,
- urban development,
- rural investment,
- resilient transportation infrastructure,
- increased capacity of health care systems,
- insurance schemes,
- uptake of innovative technologies, and
- better family and community supports.

While LMICs do not have the resources or infrastructure of higher-income countries, they do have some advantages in resiliency and adaptation, said Ailshire. Some of the most innovative adaptations come from LMICs because "they have to innovate." For example, countries without ready access to fossil fuels are investing in solar, wind, and other technologies. In addition, LMICs have the opportunity to rely on strong family and community supports, which are less common in higher-income countries.

However, she said, these supports could be weakening as family size and structure are changing over time.

Ailshire shared an example of a macro-level adaptation effort undertaken by the World Bank. Unpaved roads can become difficult or impossible to navigate after heavy rain; it may be even more difficult for people with mobility issues or women carrying children. To address this issue, the World Bank has begun improving roads in India, building a road system that is resilient to weather conditions and improves access to education, health care, and economic opportunities.[2]

There are a number of research challenges and opportunities in the area of environmental hazards and their impact on LMICs, said Ailshire. In terms of collecting data on the environment, environmental data may be sparse in LMIC settings, and administrative data typically do not have adequate coverage. However, there are opportunities for surveys to innovate—for example, by using personal air pollution monitors or having interviewers capture observations of environmental conditions. In her own work in India, she said, they are using satellite data and other systems like Google Street View to get a sense of environmental conditions and physical environments. Even with data, however, Ailshire warned that there is an additional challenge around the conceptualization of environmental effects. Risks for poor outcomes will differ across settings, and there is a need for content and context experts to think about how to measure environments and model the effects. Modeling is a challenge, particularly because environmental events can vary substantially in timing, duration, and impact, and there are synergistic effects between multiple physical and social environmental hazards and stressors. For example, air pollution may exacerbate a heat wave, and the effects on individuals may vary considerably depending on length of exposure, mobility and preexisting conditions, and ability to mitigate or adapt to an event.

DISCUSSION

Minki Chatterji (National Institute on Aging) began a wide-ranging discussion after noting that it was helpful to have pre-event data when studying the effects of the tsunami in Indonesia. Of course, "we don't know where these things are going to happen," so how do we prioritize data collection? In addition, Chatterji said that the Indonesia study is important because it demonstrated how different policies that were put into place mitigated some of the negative effects of the event. With climate change, there will be more events like this one, so there is a need to consider how to best collect data on both the event itself and policies implemented.

---

[2] https://www.worldbank.org/en/country/india/brief/connecting-villages-through-rural-roads-in-india

Emily Agree (Johns Hopkins University; workshop planning committee member) said that one important takeaway from the session was about the role of infrastructure. "Even in the best of times," lack of infrastructure affects health and well-being, and natural disasters and events can exacerbate these challenges. It is important to do the work to understand the environment and infrastructure of areas in order to assess a community's vulnerability to disasters or access to health care.

Anthony Ngugi (The Aga Khan University) asked Frankenberg whether there is a way to tap into local knowledge when studying communities. He noted that when people have lived in a place for a long time, they often have accumulated knowledge about drivers that cause health outcomes or about changes that have occurred over time. He recounted that he and his colleague encountered a group of Maasai men when scouting for research sites; the men could tell Ngugi and his colleague about how cattle grazing had changed over the last 50 years due to climate change and government actions. He asked: "How can we tap into this kind of knowledge in order to not look at these populations only as study subjects, but as people who also have knowledge that can be useful?" Frankenberg agreed with the importance of local knowledge and said that the STAR study conducted detailed community and facility interviews to talk to multiple informants at the community level. She added that the knowledge of the community is often not about "big dramatic changes" but about smaller changes over time that the local inhabitants have observed. For example, in coastal North Carolina communities, people who are often hesitant to talk about climate change are very much aware of the changes over the last 20 years in the type of shrimp that can be caught in the area.

8

Key Takeaways

In the final session of the workshop, Rebeca Wong (University of Texas Medical Branch at Galveston; workshop planning committee chair) invited each of the moderators to give a brief summary of key points from their sessions and from the workshop in general. Following these remarks, representatives of the Pan American Health Organization (PAHO) and National Institute on Aging (NIA) shared their perspectives on the workshop and on next steps. She then opened the floor to all workshop participants to share their thoughts and key takeaways.

SESSION KEY POINTS

The Role of Inequality

Socioeconomic positions, family arrangements, and environmental factors are all key determinants of health and well-being, said Yaohui Zhao (Peking University; workshop planning committee member). These are also the areas where public policies can make an impact; these actionable areas were the key focus of the workshop. Research in low- and middle-income countries (LMICs) is valuable in many ways; in particular, there are heterogeneous exposures that are useful for learning more about cause and effect. There is a need to pay more attention to external validity and transportability of findings, but these challenges can be met by collecting the right data and using the right method. There are several barriers to accessing high-quality data; these include lack of data infrastructure, lack of research capacity, changes in data sharing policies, and lack of funding for research.

Zhao identified several areas where there are opportunities for near-term action to improve research in LMICs. First, international collaboration is critical, both for sharing data and for working together on environmental issues that affect everyone. Second, there are new sources of data and new ways to leverage existing data. However, she noted that it can be difficult for users to assess the quality of data; she suggested that a role for NIA would be to assess sources of data and make the assessment publicly available. Third, there is technology for data sharing. Creating "data enclaves" in a central location, as well as in individual countries, can facilitate data sharing even with new regulations. Zhao emphasized the importance of collaborating in order to avoid duplication of efforts to create and improve data sharing technologies.

Conceptual and Methodological Barriers

One key issue, said Ayaga Bawah (University of Ghana; workshop planning committee member), is a need to collect new data, particularly longitudinal data, and combine these new data with existing data. Sources of existing data include surveys that are conducted in many of the LMICs, as well as other routine datasets. Combining data sources can allow for triangulation to get a better understanding of the issues that are being investigated. All three presenters in the session emphasized the need for training LMIC researchers, particularly in the areas of survey design, data management, data analysis, and longitudinal data analysis. Speakers also emphasized the need to build partnerships and work collaboratively in ways that include LMIC scientists in an inclusive manner. Finally, said Bawah, they all emphasized the need to recognize there is a lot of diversity within and among LMICs, and it is important to recognize the differences and to account for these in research efforts.

Research and Policy Interventions

Since the rate of population aging in LMICs has accelerated in recent years, Wong said, speakers emphasized the importance of studying future older adults (i.e., younger people) in order to detect patterns that will affect them as older adults. For example, high rates of obesity and diabetes may have serious consequences as these populations age. There is a need for longitudinal studies that collect data both before and after policies are implemented in order to measure the impact of policies. Speakers mentioned that there are policy databases in higher-income countries and that similar efforts would be very valuable for LMICs. Harmonization of data was called out as being important, but speakers also noted that it is essential to pay attention to context-specific variables and to collect data that are important, even if they cannot be harmonized with other data. Studies need to be designed in order to capture variability in exposure to the intervention (e.g., a new policy), and to enable cross-national comparisons when appropriate.

The Role of Family

In looking at LMICs, Emily Agree (Johns Hopkins University; workshop planning committee member) first stressed the importance of understanding the centrality and reliance on family caregiving for older adults with chronic illness or disability, as well as home-based care work. Within this area, she said, the speakers gave a lot of attention to understanding family caregivers and how caregiving affects their health, labor force participation, and other outcomes. It is important to look not just at individual caregivers, but also to understand care networks and how both family and nonfamily members work together to take care of older family members. In addition, family resources are an important factor when considering how unmet needs may lead to further disability and poor health.

Second, said Agree, living arrangements and social isolation are significant factors in understanding the well-being of older people in LMICs. However, there is a need for more investigation because a lot of research is imbued with assumptions about what specific living arrangements mean and who benefits from them. There is a need to dive deeper in order to understand the meaning and the value of multigenerational households, of living alone, and other living arrangements, and to identify the nuances that really reflect families' experiences.

Use of Existing Data

Wong said that the speakers emphasized conducting more research on life-course trajectories because there are limited data in this area. There was also a major emphasis on leveraging existing studies by adding aging content. Engaging with existing studies—whether longitudinal or not—presents a lower-cost opportunity to efficiently increase research on aging in LMICs.

Role of Environmental Exposures

LMICs have the greatest vulnerability to the effects of climate change, climate shocks, and environmental exposures, and older adults are among the most vulnerable within LMICs, said Mary Ganguli (University of Pittsburgh; workshop planning committee member). There are multiple levels and mechanisms through which climate factors affect health, and how factors related to aging are key to the increased vulnerability of older adults.

There are major risks from household air pollution from traditional indoor cooking and heating methods, and how it contributes to poor health in LMICs, in addition to the effects of climate change and outdoor pollution. Speakers also discussed the synergistic relationship between environmental hazards, exposure, and vulnerabilities and described opportunities and challenges for adaptation and mitigation.

PAN AMERICAN HEALTH ORGANIZATION PERSPECTIVE

Patricia Morsch (Pan American Health Organization) first offered a brief overview of the work of PAHO. PAHO works as two organizations, she said, serving as both the health organization of the inter-American system and as the regional office for the World Health Organization (WHO) in the Americas. As part of this work, PAHO provides technical coordination for the countries in the Americas on public health, working directly with ministries of health.

Morsch explained that she works in the Healthy Aging Program, the main focus of which is implementing the United Nations Decade of Healthy Aging. There are four main areas of action, she said, and these areas are very closely related to the topics discussed at the workshop:

1. protecting older adults' rights and combatting all forms of ageism;
2. promoting age-friendly environments;
3. creating or providing integrated person-centered care; and
4. long-term care.

The Decade of Healthy Aging plan acknowledges that in order to work in these areas of action, there is a need for "enablers." These enablers include increasing data information and innovation, building capacity, and increasing leadership and collaboration. All of these important ideas were discussed at the workshop, said Morsch. PAHO collaborates with many partner organizations in order to use evidence-based information to support countries in guidance, policies, and practices.

NATIONAL INSTITUTE ON AGING PERSPECTIVE

Minki Chatterji (NIA) said that the workshop was a "colossal [...] task," but it was well carried out. She said that the presentations and discussion will be enormously helpful to NIA as it builds a portfolio over the next decade to address aging.

Chatterji identified key takeaways from the workshop, divided into five categories: inequality, family, environment, data needs, and training. There is a lot of inequality not just across but also within countries, and social gradients in health are "not going to go away." What is needed, she said, is to look for policies that can mitigate the unequal negative effects on health. The research agenda at NIA needs to include research on how different policy environments can affect inequality. In terms of family structure, living arrangements, and aging, said Chatterji, it seems that a mixed-methods approach might be necessary for learning more about how family and aging interact. It is important to determine what sort of data are needed and to employ both quantitative and qualitative methods in order to capture these data in a comprehensive, nuanced way.

One particular area that seems ripe for further research is the grandparent–grandchild relationship. In the aging world, people sometimes "fall into this trap" of thinking of older adults as people who need to be taken care of, but we also need to think about older adults as people with purpose who are capable of taking care of others.

For environmental research, there is a tension between collecting the data necessary to intervene appropriately (e.g., collecting data on specific disease outbreaks, specific pollution issues) while protecting people's privacy and complying with data regulations. Chatterji said this is an issue that she is "concerned about" and that needs to be addressed.

In terms of data needs, there are 3 main approaches that could be taken: (1) start Harmonized Cognitive Assessment Protocol (HCAP) studies in new countries, (2) initiate studies in locations where data are lacking, and (3) leverage cohorts that were not originally designed to study aging. Each has its benefits and drawbacks, and all should be considered as ways to build the evidence base on aging in LMICs. Finally, she said, training was mentioned multiple times at the workshop. It is clear that there is a need for building capacity in the field and working within LMICs to train and support researchers. Chatterji closed by asking workshop participants to give feedback on what she had identified as key takeaways and to add their thoughts and perspectives on the research agenda going forward.

GENERAL DISCUSSION

Measuring Gradients

As Chatterji mentioned, social gradients in health are important to measure and understand, said Jacquiline Avila (University of Massachusetts Boston). She emphasized the importance of looking at how patterns change in gradients with each new wave of research, as this will provide even more information on the impact of interventions on inequalities. Nikki Sudharsanan (Technical University of Munich) agreed and said that it is important to measure both the absolute level of an outcome (e.g., mortality) and to look at the inequalities between groups and the gradient.

Need for Multiple Sources and Methods

The modern causal inference toolkit sets a high bar for researchers, said Sudharsanan. In research on policies, it can be very difficult to determine causation, which presents an interesting challenge when seeking funding for projects. A quasi-experimental research study designed to prospectively evaluate the impact of a policy can fail for multiple reasons outside the researcher's control, he said. The standard funding grant application to look at the effect of policies on health is inherently challenging because of the unpredictability of whether quasi-experiments would work.

Lindsay Kobayashi (University of Michigan) agreed and said that researchers need to think of quasi-experimental methods as one tool in a broad toolkit. Researchers need to consider creative methods and sources of data to evaluate policies, including observational data and linked data sources. Having a publicly available source of data on policies in order to enhance data linkages would be enormously helpful for informing robust, strong research questions and contextually grounding the work, she said.

Feinian Chen (Johns Hopkins University) agreed that mixed-methods research is necessary in this area, particularly in examining family relationships. Survey data can only "get you so far" when investigating quality of relationships and other within-family dynamics. Similarly, common tools such as time-use diaries can capture how people use their time, but they may not capture the entire experience of a caregiver's emotional and cognitive labor.

Opportunities for Research

Morsch suggested two areas in which she sees opportunities for future research. First, PAHO and WHO use the term "healthy aging," which is the ability to maintain the capacities and abilities to do what you value, she said. This definition incorporates both the environment of a person and their intrinsic capacities (e.g., cognition, locomotion). There is a group at WHO now working on measurements for healthy aging; the concepts are very broad and difficult to measure. More work is needed to determine how to best measure concepts such as "ability to participate," "having purpose," and "opportunities to grow." Second, said Morsch, PAHO uses a life-course perspective when looking at inequalities. She explained that health is something built over time as a person builds on their opportunities and capacities. Inequalities early in life can have dramatic consequences for well-being later in life; for example, people who do not have the opportunity to get an education early in life are less likely to reach their full capacity for health. Looking at inequalities in aging through a life-course perspective is an area that is ripe for future research.

Importance of Nationally Representative Data

There is a tradeoff between using data that are nationally representative and data that are fit for the purpose you need, said Hans Peter Kohler (University of Pennsylvania). All things being equal, it would be great to always have nationally representative data, but these data are more expensive and burdensome to collect. In the LMIC context, said Kohler, there is a need to build on existing studies or cohorts that are useful for answering specific questions about aging, while also making systematic investments in nationally representative data.

Training

Chatterji asked for feedback on training researchers and what methods might work best to strengthen infrastructure in LMICs. Will Dow (University of California, Berkeley) responded that it is "super important" to consider how and where researchers will receive training. He told participants about a program at Berkeley that supports fellows from East Africa. The fellows come to Berkeley for a short time, followed by trainings in East Africa. There is a continued back-and-forth, he said, rather than a "one-and-done" approach. Supporting people over a longer time period is important, but it is unclear how this might fit into a typical National Institutes of Health funding mechanism. Agree added that one training model that can work well is to develop training around specific data. This is a way of bringing people together around research questions and creating community, which can be very beneficial for all involved. This could also be helpful for NIA, she said, in terms of locating training around data that NIA are supporting.

Strengthening Research Infrastructure

Several workshop participants offered ideas on how to strengthen research infrastructure:

- Form partnerships among studies or surveys (e.g., the Health and Retirement Survey International Family of Studies) in order to agree on common data elements and harmonization to facilitate cross-national comparative work or intracountry work on key questions. (Lis Nielsen, NIA)
- Revisit the idea of leveraging existing studies, even if it requires modifying or enhancing the datasets. (John Phillips, NIA)
- Find ways to share data while conforming to country- and region-specific data privacy laws. (Phillips)

- Link aging surveys to studies conducted earlier in life in order to capture information about early life (e.g., family history) to examine nuances and variation in effects. (Agree)

Ensure Sustainability of Data Collection

"Anybody can collect one wave" of data, said Wong, but the question is whether data collections can be sustained so that they are useful. When researchers start data collection in a new country or area, it is critical to think about how it will be continued. Sustainability is a major benefit of partnering with existing longitudinal surveys that are already launched, she said.

In adjourning the workshop, Wong thanked the organizers of the workshop, the moderators, speakers, and participants.

References

AARP International. (n.d.). *The Aging Readiness and Competitiveness Report: Mexico.* https://www.aarpinternational.org/file%20library/arc/countries/full%20reports/arc-report--mexico.pdf

Andrade, F. C. (2010). Measuring the impact of diabetes on life expectancy and disability-free life expectancy among older adults in Mexico. *Journals of Gerontology, Series B: Psychological Sciences and Social Sciences, 65B*(3), 381–389. https://doi.org/10.1093/geronb/gbp119

Aranco, A., Ibarrarán, P., & Stampini, M. (2022). *Prevalence of care dependence among older persons in 26 Latin American and the Caribbean countries.* Inter-American Development Bank—IDB Technical Note; 2470. http://dx.doi.org/10.18235/0004250

Beltrán-Sánchez, H., Palloni, A., Huangfu, Y., & McEniry, M. (2022). Population-level impact of adverse early life conditions on adult healthy life expectancy in low- and middle-income countries. *Population Studies, 76*(1), 19–36. https://doi.org/10.1080/00324728.2021.1933149

Biehl, J., & Petryna, A. (Eds.). (2013). *When people come first: Critical studies in global health.* Princeton University Press.

Breilh, J. (2021). *Critical epidemiology and the people's health.* Oxford University Press.

Brinkmann, B., Davies, J. I., Witham, M. D., Harling, G., Bärnighausen, T., Bountogo, M., Siedner, M. J., Ouermi, L., Junghanns, J., Coulibaly, B., Sié, A., Payne, C. F., & Kohler, I. V. (2021). Impairment in activities of daily living and unmet need for care among older adults: A population-based study from Burkina Faso. *Journals of Gerontology, Series B: Psychological Sciences and Social Sciences, 76*(9), 1880–1892. https://doi.org/10.1093/geronb/gbab041

Capistrant, B. D., Berkman, L. F., & Glymour, M. M. (2014). Does duration of spousal caregiving affect risk of depression onset? Evidence from the Health and Retirement Study. *American Journal of Geriatric Psychiatry, 22*(8), 766–770. https://doi.org/10.1016/j.jagp.2013.01.073

Chancel, L., Piketty, T., Saez, E., & Zucman, G. (2022). *World Inequality Report 2022.* World Inequality Lab. https://wir2022.wid.world/

Ciancio, A., Behrman, J. R., Kämpfen, F., Kohler, I. V., Maurer, J., Mwapasa, V., & Kohler, H.-P. (2023). Barker's hypothesis among the global poor: Positive long-term cardiovascular effects of *in utero* famine exposure. *Demography.* https://doi.org/10.1215/00703370-11052790

Cissé, G., McLeman, R., Adams, H., Aldunce, P., Bowen, K., Campbell-Lendrum, D., Clayton, S., Ebi, K. L., Hess, J., Huang, C., Liu, Q., McGregor, G., Semenza, J., & Tirado, M. C. (2022). Health, wellbeing, and the changing structure of communities. In H.-O. Pörtner, D. C. Roberts, M. Tignor, E. S. Poloczanska, K. Mintenbeck, A. Alegría, M. Craig, S. Langsdorf, S. Löschke, V. Möller, A. Okem, & B. Rama (Eds.), *Climate Change 2022— Impacts, Adaptation and Vulnerability* (pp. 1041–1170). Contribution of Working Group II to the Sixth Assessment Report of the Intergovernmental Panel on Climate Change. Cambridge University Press. https://doi.org/10.1017/9781009325844.009

Craig, P., Katikireddi, S. V., Leyland, A., & Popham, F. (2017). Natural experiments: An overview of methods, approaches, and contributions to public health intervention research. *Annual Review of Public Health, 20*(38), 39–56. https://doi.org/10.1146/annurev-publhealth-031816-044327

Das, J., & Mohpal, Y. (2016). Socioeconomic status and quality of care in rural India: New evidence from provider and household surveys. *Health Affairs, 35*(10), 1764–1773.

Dodman, D., Hayward, B., Pelling, M., Castan Broto, V., Chow, W., Chu, E., Dawson, R., Khirfan, L., McPhearson, T., Prakash, A., Zheng, Y., & Ziervogel, G. (2022). Cities, settlements and key infrastructure. In H.-O. Pörtner, D. C. Roberts, M. Tignor, E. S. Poloczanska, K. Mintenbeck, A. Alegría, M. Craig, S. Langsdorf, S. Löschke, V. Möller, A. Okem, & B. Rama (Eds.), *Climate Change 2022—Impacts, Adaptation and Vulnerability* (pp. 1041–1170). Contribution of Working Group II to the Sixth Assessment Report of the Intergovernmental Panel on Climate Change. Cambridge University Press. https://doi.org/10.1017/9781009325844.009

Erlangga, D., Suhrcke, M., Ali, S., & Bloor, K. (2019). The impact of public health insurance on health care utilisation, financial protection and health status in low- and middle-income countries: A systematic review. *PLoS ONE, 14*(8), e0219731. https://doi.org/10.1371/journal.pone.0219731

Frankenberg, E., Lawton, R., Seeman, T. E., Sumantri, C., & Thomas, D. (2018). *The causal impact of stress on inflammation over the long-term: Evidence from exposure to a natural disaster* [Conference session]. 2019 Population Association of America Annual Meeting. Washington, DC. http://paa2019.populationassociation.org/uploads/191250

Frankenberg, E., Sikoki, B., Sumantri, C., Suriastini, W., & Thomas, D. (2023). Education, vulnerability, and resilience after a natural disaster. *Ecology & Society, 8*(2), 16. http://dx.doi.org/10.5751/ES-05377-180216

Gonçalves, N. G., Avila, J. C., Bertola, L., Michaels Obregón, A., Ferri, C. P., Wong, R., & Suemoto, C. K. (2023). Education and cognitive function among older adults in Brazil and Mexico. *Alzheimer's & Dementia: Diagnosis, Assessment & Disease Monitoring, 15*, 1–9. https://doi.org/10.1002/dad2.12470

Gupta, A., Hathi, P., Banaji, M., Gupta, P., Kashyap, R., Paikra, P., Sharma, L., Somanchi, A., Sudharsanan, N., & Vyas, S. (2023). Large and unequal life expectancy declines associated with the COVID-19 pandemic in India in 2020. https://osf.io/preprints/socarxiv/8juds

Harling, G., Kobayashi, L. C., Farrell, M. T., Wagner, R. G., Tollman, S., & Berkman, L. (2020). Social contact, social support, and cognitive health in a population-based study of middle-aged and older men and women in rural South Africa. *Social Science & Medicine (1982), 260*, 113167. https://doi.org/10.1016/j.socscimed.2020.113167

Hoang, C. T., Kohler, I. V., Amin, V., Behrman, J. R., & Kohler, H.-P. (2023). Resilience, accelerated aging and persistently poor health: Diverse trajectories of health in Malawi. *Population and Development Review.* https://doi.org/10.1111/padr.12590

Jock, J., Kobayashi, L., Chakraborty, R., Chen, X., Wing, C., Berkman, L., Canning, D., Kabudula, C. W., Tollman, S., & Rosenberg, M. (2023). Effects of pension eligibility expansion on men's cognitive function: Findings from rural South Africa. *Journal of Aging & Social Policy*, 1–20. https://doi.org/10.1080/08959420.2023.2195785

Kämpfen, F., Kohler, I. V., Bountogo, M., Mwera, J., Kohler, H. P., & Maurer, J. (2020). Using grip strength to compute physical health-adjusted old age dependency ratios. *SSM - Population Health*, *11*, 100579. https://doi.org/10.1016/j.ssmph.2020.100579

Kobayashi, L. C., Farrell, M. T., Langa, K. M., Mahlalela, N., Wagner, R. G., & Berkman, L. F. (2021). Incidence of cognitive impairment during aging in rural South Africa: Evidence from HAALSI, 2014 to 2019. *Neuroepidemiology*, *55*(2), 100–108. https://doi.org/10.1159/000513276

Kwete, X., Tang, K., Chen, L., Ren, R., Chen, Q., Wu, Z., Cai, Y., & Li, H. (2022). Decolonizing global health: What should be the target of this movement and where does it lead us? *Global Health Research and Policy*, *7*, Article 3. https://doi.org/10.1186/s41256-022-00237-3

Lagomarsino, G., Garabrant, A., Adyas, A., Muga, R., & Otoo, N. (2012). Moving towards universal health coverage: Health insurance reforms in nine developing countries in Africa and Asia. *Lancet (London, England)*, *380*(9845), 933–943. https://doi.org/10.1016/S0140-6736(12)61147-7

Lee, L., Bing, R., Kiang, J., Bashir, S., Spath, N., Stelzle, D., Mortimer, K., Bularga, A., Doudesis, D., Joshi, S., Strachan, F., Gumy, S., Adair-Rohani, H., Attia, E., Chung, M., Miller, M., Newby, D., Mills, N., McAllister, D., & Shah, A. (2020). Adverse health effects associated with household air pollution: A systematic review, meta-analysis, and burden estimation study. *Lancet Global Health*, *8*, e1427–e1434. https://doi.org/10.1016/S2214-109X(20)30343-0

Li, J., Lin, S., Yan, X., Wei, Y., Yang, F., & Pei, L. (2023). Cross-country comparison of income-related inequality in physical functional disability among middle-aged and older adults: Evidence from 33 countries. *Journal of Global Health*, *13*, 04053. https://doi.org/10.7189/jogh.13.04053

Limwattananon, S., Tangcharoensathien, V., & Prakongsai, P. (2007). Catastrophic and poverty impacts of health payments: Results from national household surveys in Thailand. *Bulletin of the World Health Organization*, *85*(8), 600–606. https://doi.org/10.2471/blt.06.033720

Lin, L., Wang, H. H., Lu, C., Chen, W., & Guo, V. Y. (2021). Adverse childhood experiences and subsequent chronic diseases among middle-aged or older adults in China and associations with demographic and socioeconomic characteristics. *JAMA Network Open*, *4*(10), e2130143. https://doi.org/10.1001/jamanetworkopen.2021.30143. Erratum in: (2022). *JAMA Network Open*, *5*(6), e2220614. https://doi.org/10.1001/jamanetworkopen.2022.20614

Mohanty, S. K., Upadhyay, A. K., Maiti S., Mishra, R. S., Kämpfen, F., Maurer, J., & O'Donnell, O. (2023). Public health insurance coverage in India before and after PM-JAY: Repeated cross-sectional analysis of nationally representative survey data. *BMJ Global Health*, *8*(8), 1–12.

National Academies of Sciences, Engineering, and Medicine (National Academies). (2021). *High and rising mortality rates among working-age adults*. The National Academies Press. https://doi.org/10.17226/25976

———. (2022). *Structural racism and rigorous models of social inequity: Proceedings of a workshop*. The National Academies Press. https://doi.org/10.17226/26690

Organisation for Economic Co-operation and Development. (2023). *Old-age dependency ratio (indicator)*. https://doi.org/10.1787/e0255c98-en

Palloni, A., & Beltran-Sanchez, H. (2017). The impact of obesity on adult mortality: Assessment of estimates with applications (RAND Working Paper Series WR-1193). *SSRN.* http://dx.doi.org/10.2139/ssrn.2985856

Palloni, A., McEniry M., Huangfu Y., and Beltran-Sanchez, H. (2020). Impacts of the 1918 flu on survivors' nutritional status: A double quasi-natural experiment. *PLoS ONE, 15*(10), e0232805. https://doi.org/10.1371/journal.pone.0232805

Parati, G., Ochoa, J. E., & Lackland, D. T. (2023). Easier access to antihypertensive treatment: The key for improving blood pressure control in sub-Saharan Africa? *Hypertension (Dallas, Tex.: 1979), 80*(8), 1624–1627. https://doi.org/10.1161/HYPERTENSIONAHA.123.20872

Parker, S. W., Saenz, J., & Wong, R. (2018). Health insurance and the aging: Evidence from the Seguro Popular Program in Mexico. *Demography, 55*(1), 361–386. https://doi.org/10.1007/s13524-017-0645-4

Payne, C. F. (2018). Aging in the Americas: Disability-free life expectancy among adults aged 65 and older in the United States, Costa Rica, Mexico, and Puerto Rico. *Journals of Gerontology, Series B: Psychological Sciences and Social Sciences, 73*(2), 337–348. https://doi.org/10.1093/geronb/gbv076

Payne, C. F. (2022). Expansion, compression, neither, both? Divergent patterns in healthy, disability-free, and morbidity-free life expectancy across U.S. birth cohorts, 1998–2016. *Demography, 59*(3), 949–973. https://doi.org/10.1215/00703370-9938662

Payne, C. F., & Wong, R. (2019). Expansion of disability across successive Mexican birth cohorts: A longitudinal modelling analysis of birth cohorts born 10 years apart. *Journal of Epidemiology and Community Health, 73*(10), 900–905. https://doi.org/10.1136/jech-2019-212245

Payne, C. F., Liwin, L. K., Wade, A. N., Houle, B., Du Toit, J. D., Flood, D., & Manne-Goehler, J. (2023). Impact of diabetes on longevity and disability-free life expectancy among older South African adults: A prospective longitudinal analysis. *Diabetes Research and Clinical Practice, 197*, 110577. https://doi.org/10.1016/j.diabres.2023.110577

Pradhan, E., Suzuki, E. M., Martínez, S., Schäferhoff, M., & Jamison, D. T. (2017). The effects of education quantity and quality on child and adult mortality: Their magnitude and their value. In D. A. P. Bundy, N. D. Silva, S. Horton, D. T. Jamison, & G. C. Patton (Eds.), *Child and adolescent health and development, 3rd ed.* The International Bank for Reconstruction and Development, The World Bank.

Prina, A. M., Wu, Y. T., Kralj, C., Acosta, D., Acosta, I., Guerra, M., Huang, Y., Jotheeswaran, A. T., Jimenez-Velazquez, I. Z., Liu, Z., Llibre Rodriguez, J. J., Salas, A., Sosa, A. L., & Prince, M. (2020). Dependence- and disability-free life expectancy across eight low- and middle-income countries: A 10/66 study. *Journal of Aging and Health, 32*(5-6), 401–409. https://doi.org/10.1177/0898264319825767

Reubi, D. (2018). Epidemiological accountability: Philanthropists, global health and the audit of saving lives. *Economy and Society, 47*(1), 83–110. https://doi.org/10.1080/03085147.2018.1433359

Rivera-Hernandez, M., Rahman, M., Mor, V., & Galarraga, O. (2016). The impact of social health insurance on diabetes and hypertension process indicators among older adults in Mexico. *Health Services Research, 51*(4), 1323–1346. https://doi.org/10.1111/1475-6773.12404

Rosenberg, M., Beidelman, E., Chen, X., Canning, D., Kobayashi, L., Kahn, K., Pettifor, A., & Whiteson Kabudula, C. (2023). The impact of a randomized cash transfer intervention on mortality of adult household members in rural South Africa, 2011–2022. *Social Science & Medicine, 324*(115883). https://doi.org/10.1016/j.socscimed.2023.115883.

Rosero-Bixby, L., & Dow, W. H. (2016). Exploring why Costa Rica outperforms the United States in life expectancy: A tale of two inequality gradients. *Proceedings of the National Academy of Sciences of the United States of America, 113*(5), 1130–1137. https://doi.org/10.1073/pnas.1521917112

Rowe, J. W. (2015). Successful aging of societies. *Dædalus*, *44*(2), 5–11.

Saenz, J., Adar, S. D., Zhang, Y., Wilkens, J., Chattopadhyay, A., Lee, J., & Wong, R. (2021). Household use of polluting cooking fuels and late-life cognitive function: A harmonized analysis of India, Mexico, and China. *Environment International*, *156*(106722). https://doi.org/10.1016/j.envint.2021.106722

Smith, J. P. (2009). Reconstructing childhood health histories. *Demography*, *46*(2), 387–403. https://doi.org/10.1353/dem.0.0058

Sousa, R. M., Ferri, C. P., Acosta, D., Albanese, E., Guerra, M., Huang, Y., Jacob, K. S., Jotheeswaran, A. T., Rodriguez, J. J., Pichardo, G. R., Rodriguez, M. C., Salas, A., Sosa, A. L., Williams, J., Zuniga, T., & Prince, M. (2009). Contribution of chronic diseases to disability in elderly people in countries with low and middle incomes: A 10/66 Dementia Research Group population-based survey. *Lancet (London, England)*, *374*(9704), 1821–1830. https://doi.org/10.1016/S0140-6736(09)61829-8

Torres, J. M., Rizzo, S., & Wong, R. (2018). Lifetime socioeconomic status and late-life health trajectories: Longitudinal results from the Mexican Health and Aging Study. *Journals of Gerontology, Series B: Psychological Sciences and Social Sciences*, *73*(2), 349–360. https://doi.org/10.1093/geronb/gbw048

Xu, K. Q., Aw, J., & Payne, C. F. (2023, April 12–15). *Inequality in healthy life expectancy in the Asia-Pacific: A cross-national analysis* [Conference session]. PAA Annual Meeting. New Orleans, LA. https://events.rdmobile.com/Asset/Download/3a291d46-577a-4130-bbc3-405aeadffb60

Yam, E. A., Silva, M., Ranganathan, M., White, J., Hope, T. M., & Ford, C. L. (2021). Time to take critical race theory seriously: Moving beyond a colour-blind gender lens in global health. *Lancet Global Health*, *9*(4), e389–e390. https://doi.org/10.1016/S2214-109X(20)30536-2

Yao, Y., Wang, K., & Xiang, H. (2022). Association between cognitive function and ambient particulate matters in middle-aged and elderly Chinese adults: Evidence from the China Health and Retirement Longitudinal Study (CHARLS). *Science of the Total Environment*, *828*, 154297. https://doi.org/10.1016/j.scitotenv.2022.154297

Zhang, B., Weuve, J., Langa, K. M., D'Souza, J., Szpiro, A., Faul, J., Mendes de Leon, C., Gao, J., Kaufman, J. D., Sheppard, L., Lee, J., Kobayashi, L. C., Hirth, R., & Adar, S. D. (2023). Comparison of particulate air pollution from different emission sources and incident dementia in the U.S. *JAMA Internal Medicine*, *183*(10), 1080–1089. https://doi.org/10.1001/jamainternmed.2023.3300

Appendix A

Workshop Agenda

WORKSHOP ON DEVELOPING AN AGENDA FOR
POPULATION AGING AND SOCIAL RESEARCH IN
LOW- AND MIDDLE-INCOME COUNTRIES (LMICS)
September 7–8, 2023

Workshop Goals: to identify the most promising directions for behavioral and social research and data infrastructure investments for studying life course health, aging, and Alzheimer's disease and related dementias in low- and middle-income countries (LMICs).

Agenda

DAY 1: Thursday, September 7, 2023, 9:30am–3:30pm ET

All sessions open to the public
National Academy of Sciences Building, Room 120 and webcast

9:30am–10:00am   Welcome and introductory remarks from the planning committee and National Institute on Aging

Rebeca Wong (University of Texas Medical Branch at Galveston, workshop planning committee chair)

Amy Kelley (National Institute on Aging), *virtual participant*
Lis Nielsen (National Institute on Aging), *virtual participant*
Minki Chatterji (National Institute on Aging)

10:00am–10:20am   Keynote/setting the stage

Lisa Berkman (Harvard University)

10:20am–11:40am   Session 1: How inequality (income, wealth, access to opportunities or resources) affects health and well-being of older populations in LMICs

Presenters:
Jaqueline Contrera-Avila (University of Massachusetts Boston)
Nikkil Sudharsanan (Technical University of Munich)

Discussant:
Will Dow (University of California, Berkeley), *virtual participant*

Moderator:
Yaohui Zhao (Peking University; workshop planning committee member)

Guiding Questions:
How does income inequality affect health and well-being of older populations in LMICs in the context of changing and evolving economies?
How are changes in the nature of work influencing disability, dementia, and mortality?
Are there trends, are they actionable?

11:40am–12:35pm   Lunch Break

12:35pm–1:55pm   Session 2: Identify new conceptual, theoretical, methodological, and/or data investments that are needed to move from purely descriptive cross-national analyses to more causal analyses that create a better understanding of how inequality, environmental exposures, and changing family structures impact health and well-being at older ages in LMICs.

Presenters:
Hiram Beltrán-Sánchez (University of California, Los Angeles)
Sam Clark (The Ohio State University)

Discussant:
Hans Peter Kohler (University of Pennsylvania)

Moderator:
Ayaga Bawah (University of Ghana, workshop planning committee member)

Guiding Question:
What methods should we consider/promote for causal analyses using cross-national data?

1:55pm–2:10pm   Break

2:10pm–3:30pm   Session 3: Describe how research in LMICs can (1) create a better understanding of how different social environments and public policies influence health outcomes related to aging; and (2) provide lessons that can be used in other settings, including the United States.

Presenters:
Collin Payne (Australian National University)
David Canning (Harvard University)

Discussant:
Lindsay Kobayashi (University of Michigan)

Moderator:
Rebeca Wong (University of Texas Medical Branch at Galveston, workshop planning committee chair)

Guiding Questions:
What types of policy interventions, such as those related to pensions, long-term care, formal and

informal care, influence health and the well-being of older populations in LMICs?

What types of lessons does this provide for other countries, including the United States?

3:30pm ET   Adjournment

DAY 2: Friday, September 8, 2023, 9:00am–3:30pm ET

All sessions open to the public
National Academy of Sciences Building, Room 120 and webcast

9:00am–9:15am   Welcome, brief recap of Day 1

9:15am–10:35am   Session 4: How family changes affect the health and well-being of older populations in LMICs.

Presenters:
Pablo Ibarrarán (Inter-American Development Bank), *virtual participant*
Feinian Chen (Johns Hopkins University)

Discussant:
Carmen García Peña (Instituto Nacional de Geriatria, Mexico), *virtual participant*

Moderator:
Emily Agree (Johns Hopkins University, workshop planning committee member)

Guiding Questions:
How do changes in household composition, family size, and time to marriage affect health and well-being of older populations in LMICs?

10:35am–10:50am   Break

10:50am–12:10pm   Session 5: Identify data (e.g., early-life prospective data or retrospective data from current older cohorts; data linkages, or leverage existing cohorts established for other non-aging purposes) that may

be of interest for examining life-course trajectories
of development and aging in LMICs.

Presenters:
Amparo Palacios-López (World Bank), *virtual
participant*
Anthony Ngugi (The Aga Khan University)

Discussant:
Andrew Steptoe (University College London*),
virtual participant*

Moderator:
David Weir (University of Michigan, planning
committee member)

Guiding Questions:
What administrative linkages should we consider to
enhance the utility of existing data?
How can we continue to foster data sharing and
deal with data sharing issues?
What existing cohort studies might be used as
samples for longitudinal studies of aging?
What administrative linkages are available to
enhance existing data or complement new studies?
What sampling frames (including administrative
data as well as censuses, etc.) are available to lower
the cost of finding potential participants?
What data sharing challenges do we face and what
solutions are available?

12:10pm–1:00pm   Lunch Break

1:00pm–2:20pm   Session 6: How environmental exposure affects
                   health and well-being of older populations in
                   LMICs

                   Presenters:
                   Sara Adar (University of Michigan)
                   Elizabeth Frankenberg (University of North
                   Carolina), *virtual participant*

Discussant:
Jennifer Ailshire (University of Southern California)

Moderator:
Mary Ganguli (University of Pittsburgh, workshop planning committee member)

Guiding Questions:
What are the mechanisms through which exposures operate?
What adaptation and mitigation strategies have been or need to be developed to reduce the harmful effects of environmental exposure?
To what extent are the impacts of exposure on health outcomes specific to LMICs, given their country-specific contexts?

2:20pm–2:35pm   Break

2:35–3:30pm   Roundtable discussion and Q&A
Members of the planning committee, representatives from NIA, and workshop attendees will discuss key takeaways.

Moderator:
Rebeca Wong (University of Texas Medical Branch at Galveston, workshop planning committee chair)

3:30pm   Adjournment

Appendix B

Biographical Sketches for Workshop Planning Committee Members and Speakers

SARA ADAR (she/her/hers) is an associate professor and associate chair of the Department of Epidemiology at the University of Michigan School of Public Health. Currently, she has a large research portfolio on environmental risk factors of accelerated aging funded by the National Institutes of Health, and she is a multiple principal investigator of the National Institute on Aging–funded Gateway to Global Aging project. Adar has won awards for her teaching from the University of Michigan and for her research from the American Heart Association and the International Society for Environmental Epidemiology. She is currently a member of the Review Committee for the Health Effects Institute, an associate editor of *Environmental Health Perspectives*, and a standing member of the Cardiovascular and Respiratory Disease Study Section for the National Institutes of Health. She holds a B.S. in environmental engineering from the Massachusetts Institute of Technology, an M.H.S. from the Johns Hopkins Bloomberg School of Public Health, and an Sc.D. from the Harvard T.H. Chan School of Public Health.

EMILY M. AGREE (workshop planning committee member, she/her/hers) is research professor at Johns Hopkins University and associate director of the Hopkins Population Center. She previously served as director of the Hopkins Center for Population Aging and Health. Her research expertise is on disability and long-term care, aging families, and intergenerational relationships. Agree is a member of the steering committee for the National Health and Aging Trends Study, a nationally representative longitudinal study of disability in later life. Her work has focused on the relationship

115

of assistive technology use to disability in later life and the influence of population aging on family relationships and old-age support. She has served on the Population Association of America Board of Directors and the editorial boards of *Demography*, and the *Journal of Gerontology: Social Sciences, and Research on Aging*. Agree holds an M.A. in demography from Georgetown University and Ph.D. in sociology from Duke University. She currently serves on National Academies of Sciences, Engineering, and Medicine's Committee on Population.

JENNIFER AILSHIRE (she/her/hers) is associate professor of gerontology, associate dean of research and associate dean of international programs and global initiatives at the Leonard Davis School of Gerontology at the University of Southern California (USC). Her research has demonstrated the importance of physical and social environments, and their interactions, in determining health and well-being across the adult life course, and particularly for older adults. Ailshire is the architect of the Contextual Data Resource, which can be linked to longitudinal studies of aging in the United States to facilitate examination of socioenvironmental determinants of health and aging. She is a co-director of the USC/University of California, Los Angeles' Center on Biodemography and Population Health and co-investigator on the Gateway to Global Aging. Ailshire's research on global aging focuses on health and cognition, social inequality, and caregiving, and she is currently conducting a pilot study of aging in Colombia. She holds a Ph.D. in sociology, with a specialization in demography, from the University of Michigan.

JAQUELINE C. AVILA (she/her/hers) is an assistant professor in the Department of Gerontology at the University of Massachusetts Boston. She is an early-stage investigator interested in social determinants of older adult health in Latin America. Avila has published several papers on the health of older Mexican adults using data from the Mexican Health and Aging Study, as well as cross-national comparisons of cognitive function between Mexico and the United States. She is currently studying how tobacco use impacts cognitive function among older adults in low- and middle-income countries. Avila completed a postdoctoral fellowship in substance use research at Brown University School of Public Health and a Ph.D. in population health sciences at the University of Texas Medical Branch.

AYAGA A. BAWAH (workshop planning committee member, he/him/his) is associate professor and director of the Regional Institute for Population Studies at the University of Ghana, and a research affiliate of the Population Studies Center, University of Pennsylvania. Prior to joining the University of Ghana, he was assistant professor at the Mailman School of Public Health at Columbia University. Bawah has expertise in population and health research in Africa, particularly in research methodology, longitudinal data analysis and modeling of demographic processes, evaluation of health interventions, fertility and reproductive health programs including family planning. He has published widely in several top-tier peer-reviewed journals and contributed several book chapters in the fields of population and health. Bawah is a member of Ghana's Food and Drugs Authority's Technical Advisory Committee on Clinical Trials, a member of the International Union for the Scientific Study of Population, the Union for African Population Studies, and the Population Association of America. He holds a B.A. in geography and resource development and an M.A. in population studies from University of Ghana, and an M.A. and Ph.D. in demography from the University of Pennsylvania. Bawah previously served on the National Academies of Sciences, Engineering, and Medicine's Committee on Continuing Epidemiological Transition in Sub-Saharan Africa from 2010 to 2013.

HIRAM BELTRÁN-SÁNCHEZ (he/him/his) is associate professor in the Department of Community Health Sciences at the Fielding School of Public Health and associate director of the California Center for Population Research at the University of California, Los Angeles. His research focuses on the demography of health and aging. Beltrán-Sánchez has written on health patterns and trends in low- and middle-income countries; on aging in high-income countries including issues about compression of morbidity; on the links between early-life experiences and late-life outcomes; as well as on biomarker data from Mexico to study physiological patterns of health and their link with sociodemographic factors. He is currently serving on the Population Association of America (PAA) Board of Directors and received the 2018 Early Achievement Award from PAA. Beltrán-Sánchez holds an M.Sc. in mathematics from Northern Arizona University, an M.A. in demography, and Ph.D. in demography from the University of Pennsylvania.

LISA F. BERKMAN (she/her/hers) is the director of the Harvard Center for Population and Development Studies, Thomas D. Cabot Professor of Public Policy, Epidemiology, and Global Health and Population, School of Public Health. She is the principal investigator of the Health and Aging Study in Africa: A Longitudinal Study of an INDEPTH Community in South Africa program—a project funded by the National Institute on Aging. Berkman co-edited (with Ichiro Kawachi) *Social Epidemiology*, a groundbreaking textbook on this burgeoning field with a second edition being published later. Her research is aimed at understanding inequalities in health related to socioeconomic status, social networks with an emphasis on workplace conditions, and labor policy. Berkman is the current president of the Population Association of America, past president of the American Population Centers, and a member of the National Academy of Medicine.

DAVID CANNING (he/him/his) is the Richard Saltonstall Professor of Population Science and professor of economics and international health in the Department of Global Health and Population at Harvard T.H. Chan School of Public Health. His research focuses on the role of demographic change (e.g., the effect of changes in age structure on aggregate economic activity) and health improvements (e.g., health as a form of human capital and its impact on worker productivity) in economic development. Canning served as associate director of the Harvard Center for Population and Development Studies and was primary investigator on the Welfare Effects of Balancing the Federal Social Security and Health Care Budgets project. He received his B.S. in mathematics and economics from Queen's University Belfast and his Ph.D. in economics from the University of Cambridge.

FEINIAN CHEN (she/her/hers) is a professor of sociology and director of the Hopkins Population Center at Johns Hopkins University. Prior to joining Johns Hopkins University, she was a professor of sociology at the University of Maryland and a faculty associate at the Maryland Population Research Center. Chen's main research interests include intergenerational relations, gender, work and family, population aging, and health. Her work is globally situated and is actively engaged in research on family transitions, gender dynamics, and their health implications in the diverse contexts of China, India, the Philippines, and the United States. Chen is currently serving as a deputy editor for *Demography* and chair for the Asia and Asian America Section of the American Sociological Association. She has served as an associate editor for the *Journal of Gerontology: Social Sciences* and the editorial boards of journals including *American Sociological Review*, *Social Forces*, *Chinese Sociological Review*, *Population Research and Policy Review*, and *Research on Aging*. Chen received her Ph.D. in sociology from the University of North Carolina at Chapel Hill and was trained in social demography at the Carolina Population Center.

SAMUEL CLARK is a professor appointed in the Department of Sociology at The Ohio State University. Clark worked for about a decade in close collaboration with statisticians at the University of Washington to develop new methods for population estimation and projection/forecasting for the United Nations' Population Division. He leads the openVA team that develops new statistical methods to automate cause of death classification using verbal autopsy interview data; contributes to developing global standards for verbal autopsy; works to improve the verbal autopsy interview; and develops and disseminates user-friendly software to integrate verbal autopsy cause of death assessment into civil registration and vital statistics systems in low- or middle-income countries. Clark is a standing member of the World Health Organization's Verbal Autopsy Reference Group. His work is supported by the National Institutes of Health, the Bill and Melinda Gates Foundation, and the Bloomberg Philanthropies through the Data for Health Initiative. Clark has a B.S. in biology and engineering from the California Institute of Technology and both an M.S. and a Ph.D. in demography from the University of Pennsylvania.

WILLIAM H. DOW (he/him/his) is a professor at the University of California, Berkeley, with appointments in the School of Public Health and the Department of Demography. He directs University of California, Berkeley's Center on the Economics and Demography of Aging and is a research associate at the National Bureau of Economic Research. Dow was principal investigator of the Costa Rican Longevity and Healthy Aging Study, is currently principal investigator of the Caribbean American Dementia and Aging Study, and is collaborating on population aging research in East Africa and East Asia. Honors include the Kenneth J. Arrow Award given by the International Health Economics Association. He holds a Ph.D. in economics from Yale University. Previously, Dow served on the steering committee for the National Academies of Sciences, Engineering, and Medicine's Workshop on Strengthening the Scientific Foundation for Policymaking to Meet the Challenges of Aging in Latin America and the Caribbean.

ELIZABETH FRANKENBERG (she/her/hers) is the Cary C. Boshamer Distinguished Professor of Sociology and the director of the Carolina Center for Population Aging and Health at the University of North Carolina at Chapel Hill. Her research focuses on individual and family response to change and the role of community, broadly construed, in individual behaviors and outcomes across the life course. Frankenberg has developed and implemented innovative and ambitious designs for data collection to support her own research and that of the scientific and policy communities more broadly, including the Study of the Tsunami Aftermath and Recovery and the Dynamics of Extreme Events, People, and Places project. She received her M.P.A. in public affairs from Princeton University and her Ph.D. in demography and sociology from the University of Pennsylvania.

MARY GANGULI (workshop planning committee member, she/her/hers) is professor of psychiatry, neurology, and epidemiology, University of Pittsburgh School of Medicine and School of Public Health, and is a medical staff member of the University of Pittsburgh Medical Center. She has conducted several National Institute on Aging–funded population-based research projects on cognitive impairment and dementia in the United States and India, where she led a large study of the epidemiology of dementia, developing screening tools for the assessment of illiterate Hindi-speaking older adults. Ganguli served on the National Advisory Council on Aging, the DSM-5 Neurocognitive Disorders work group of the American Psychiatric Association, the American Academy of Neurology Practice Parameter work groups on Mild Cognitive Impairment, and on several editorial boards of journals. She received the Distinguished Scientist Award of the American Association of Geriatric Psychiatry and the Outstanding Academician Award of the Indo-American Psychiatric Association. Ganguli holds an M.D. from Madras University, underwent psychiatry training at Memorial University of Newfoundland and the University of Pittsburgh, and holds an M.P.H. in psychiatric epidemiology from the University of Pittsburgh. She is certified in general psychiatry by the Royal College of Physicians of Canada, and in both general and geriatric psychiatry by the American Board of Psychiatry and Neurology.

CARMEN GARCÍA-PEÑA (she/her/hers) is currently the general director at the Instituto Nacional de Geriatria (National Institute of Geriatrics) in México. She is national researcher level III by the National Council of Science and Technology. García-Peña's research expertise is on aging epidemiology and public health, particularly mental health, social determinants, and how and why we age as we do. She is an active member of the National Academy of Medicine in Mexico, the Mexican Academy of Sciences, and an international member of the National Academy of Medicine in the United States. García-Peña received her M.D. with a specialty in family medicine, an M.A. in medical sciences, and a Ph.D. in public health and aging from the London School of Hygiene and Tropical Medicine.

PABLO IBARRARÁN (he/him/his) is head of the Social Protection and Health Division of the Inter-American Development Bank. He joined the bank as an evaluation economist in the Office of Evaluation and Oversight and also worked as lead economics specialist in the Office of Strategic Planning and Development Effectiveness. Ibarrarán has worked in the design, implementation, and evaluation of redistributive and social inclusion programs, as well as in the aging agenda. He has also participated in the preparation and evaluation of health programs, and is a research associate at the Institute of Labor in Bonn, Germany. Ibarrarán received his B.S. in economics from the Center for Economic Research and Teaching and his Ph.D. in economics from the University of California, Berkeley.

LINDSAY C. KOBAYASHI (she/her/hers) is the John G. Searle Assistant Professor of Epidemiology and assistant professor of global public health at the University of Michigan School of Public Health. She is the co-director of the Center for Social Epidemiology and Population Health at the University of Michigan School of Public Health and is an honorary senior researcher at the MRC/Wits Rural Health and Health Transitions Research Unit (Agincourt) at the University of the Witwatersrand in South Africa. Kobayashi currently leads research funded by the United States' National Institute on Aging to link complementary data sources on socioeconomic conditions, social policies, and cash transfers in relation to cognitive aging outcomes in rural South Africa, and to examine the consistency of associations of key dementia risk factors with later-life cognitive function across diverse global settings using cross-nationally harmonized measures of cognitive function. She holds a Ph.D. in epidemiology and public health from University College London and completed a David E. Bell postdoctoral fellowship at the Harvard Center for Population and Development Studies.

HANS-PETER KOHLER (he/him/his) is the F.J. Warren Professor of Demography and co-director of the Population Aging and Research Center at the University of Pennsylvania. He has widely published on topics related to global aging, life-course perspectives on health, fertility, social and sexual networks, HIV/AIDS, and biodemography. He directs the National Institute on Aging– and National Institute of Child Health and Human Development–funded Malawi Longitudinal Study of Families and Health, that documents more than 25 years of demographic, socioeconomic, and health conditions in one of the world's poorest countries. Kohler has been awarded the Clifford C. Clogg Award for Early Career Achievement by the Population Association of America and Otis Dudley Duncan Award for Outstanding Scholarship in Social Demography by the American Sociological Association. He received his M.A. in demography and Ph.D. in economics from the University of California, Berkeley.

PATRICIA MORSCH (she/her/hers) is a healthy aging advisor in the Department of Health Systems and Services at the Pan American Health Organization headquarters in Washington, D.C., which is the World Health Organization's regional office for the Americas. Morsch is also a physical therapist and has combined experience in clinical physical therapy and research on aging, older adults' health, and public health. Morsch worked previously in clinical and physiotherapeutic care, with an emphasis on the care of older people, at the Department of Aging of Cabarrus County, North Carolina, and as a university professor and researcher in Brazil. She holds a graduate certificate in public health, an M.A. in gerontology from the University of North Carolina at Charlotte, and a Ph.D. in biomedical gerontology from the Pontifical Catholic University of de Rio Grande do Sul.

ANTHONY NGUGI (he/him/his) is an associate professor of epidemiology and population health and interim chair for the Department of Population Health at the Aga Khan University in Kenya. He has experience in health research and has conducted large multicountry population-based studies of the epidemiology of epilepsy in Sub-Saharan Africa, set up community-level data platforms, and led large data-intensive projects in reproductive, maternal, newborn and child health (RMNCH). Ngugi is a co–primary investigator of a National Institute on Aging– and National Institutes of Health–funded Longitudinal Study of Health and Ageing in Kenya, is a member of the International Epidemiological Association, Health Systems Global, and the Nutrition Information Technical Working Group in Kenya. He has also served as a board chair for Foundation for People with Epilepsy and a board member at the National Epilepsy Coordination Committee in Kenya. Ngugi holds a B.S. in veterinary medicine, an M.S. in epidemiology and economics from the University of Nairobi, and a Ph.D. and postgraduate diploma in epidemiology and population health, both from the London School of Hygiene and Tropical Medicine.

AMPARO PALACIOS-LÓPEZ (she/her/hers) is a senior economist for the Living Standards Measurement Study, the World Bank's flagship household survey program housed at the Development Data Group. Her primary area of research is development, with a focus on labor, gender, and welfare. The recent focus of Palacios-López's methodological research has been on labor and gender, working jointly with the Gender Group of the World Bank and the International Labor Organization. As a member of the Living Standards Measurement Study team, she supports surveys in several countries of Sub-Saharan Africa and leads the design of questionnaires used in surveys in Latin America, Asia, and the Middle East. Palacios-López is part of the team of coordinators of the World Bank Household Survey Working Group and its Technical Review Panel. She received an M.A. in economics from the Pontificia Universidad Católica de Chile and a Ph.D. in development economics from the University of Maryland, College Park.

COLLIN PAYNE (he/him/his) is an associate professor of demography at the Australian National University, and a visiting faculty member at the Harvard Center for Population and Development Studies. His research focuses on key issues facing populations around the world—how long we live, how health is maintained across the life course, and how differences in healthy longevity arise both between individuals and across nations. Payne's research outputs have generated new knowledge on international patterns of social, economic, and demographic inequalities in health, demonstrating that many well-established relationships observed in high-income populations (such as the age pattern of depressive symptoms, the connections between biomarkers of health and reported disability, or the compression of morbidity with rising life expectancy) do not necessarily generalize to nonwealthy countries, or to disadvantaged subgroups within populations. His current projects include an Australian Research Council–funded study estimating and comparing health expectancies across the Asia-Pacific, and an Australian National University's Futures Scheme project developing methods for estimating the direct contributions of chronic diseases to shortfalls in healthy longevity. Payne is an Australian Research Council Discovery Early Career Researcher Award fellow. He holds a B.A. in sociology from the University of Wisconsin and a Ph.D. in demography from the University of Pennsylvania.

ANDREW STEPTOE (he/him/his) is professor of psychology and epidemiology at University College London, where he is head of the Department of Behavioural Science and Health, and director of the English Longitudinal Study of Ageing (ELSA). He was British Heart Foundation Professor of Psychology and director of the Institute of Epidemiology and Health Care at University College London. Steptoe's research is primarily focused on links between psychological and social processes and physical health, and on population ageing. He is a fellow of the British Academy, the Academy of Medical Sciences, the Royal Society of Biology, and the Academy for Social Sciences. Steptoe graduated in natural sciences from Cambridge University and completed his Ph.D. at the University of Oxford.

NIKKIL SUDHARSANAN (he/him/his) is the Rudolf Mößbauer Assistant Professor of Behavioral Science for Disease Prevention and Health Care at the Technical University of Munich. His primary expertise is on aging and mortality in low- and middle-income countries with a focus on older adults' health behaviors and beliefs, and designing and evaluating interventions for preventing cardiovascular diseases. Prior to joining the Technical University of Munich, Sudharsanan was an Alexander von Humboldt Postdoctoral Fellow at the Heidelberg Institute of Global Health and a David E. Bell Postdoctoral Fellow at the Harvard Center for Population and Development Studies. He holds an M.A. in statistics and a Ph.D. in population studies from the University of Pennsylvania. Sudharsanan previously contributed to the National Academies of Sciences, Engineering, and Medicine Workshop on the Future Directions for the Demography of Aging.

DAVID R. WEIR (workshop planning committee member, he/him/his) is research professor in the Survey Research Center of the Institute for Social Research at the University of Michigan, where he is also director of the Health and Retirement Study. He has previously held positions at Yale University and the University of Chicago. Weir's primary areas of expertise are aging and survey research, with specific training in economics and demography. He has conducted studies on population-based international comparisons of dementia and cognitive impairment, and social disparities in biomarkers of aging. Weir is a member of the National Institute on Aging's National Council on Aging, the International Union for the Scientific Study of Population, and the Population Association of America. He holds an A.B. in history from the University of Michigan and a Ph.D. in economics from Stanford University. Weir previously served on several National Academies of Sciences, Engineering, and Medicine activities, including the Committee on Population, and as the co-chair of the Planning Committee for a Workshop on Priorities for Strengthening the Scientific Foundation for Policymaking to Meet the Challenges of Aging in Latin America.

REBECA WONG (workshop planning committee chair, she/her/hers) is Sheridan Lorenz Distinguished Professor in Aging and Health; professor, Department of Population Health and Health Disparities; director, World Health Organization/Pan American Health Organization's Collaborating Center on Aging and Health; co-director, Claude Pepper Older American Independence Center, and interim director, Sealy Center on Aging—all affiliated with the University of Texas Medical Branch at Galveston. She also serves as principal investigator of the Mexican Health and Aging Study, financed by the National Institute on Aging. Wong has previously served in the faculty of the Johns Hopkins School of Public Health, Georgetown University Department of Demography, and as associate director of the University of Maryland Population Research Center. She has pioneered the use of cross-national approaches to study health outcomes including physical and cognitive function in immigrant populations, and has completed recent work on indoor air pollution and its impact on cognitive aging, socioeconomic gradients of health, economic consequences of health shocks, co-existence of infectious and chronic diseases, and the impact of the social security and health care reform among older adults in Mexico. Wong served on the National Academies of Sciences, Engineering, and Medicine's Committee on Population and was a co-chair of the Planning Committee for a Workshop on Priorities for Strengthening the Scientific Foundation for Policymaking to Meet the Challenges of Aging in Latin America.

YAOHUI ZHAO (workshop planning committee member, she/her/hers) is Yangtze River Scholar Professor of Economics at the National School of Development and the Institute for Global Health and Development of Peking University. She has been the principal investigator of the China Health and Retirement Longitudinal Study and is associate director of the Institute of Social Science Surveys of Peking University. Zhao has published more than a hundred research articles covering the fields of labor economics, health economics, and the economics of aging. She was chair of *The Path to Healthy Ageing in China: A Peking University–Lancet Commission* (2022). Zhao holds a B.A. and M.A. in economics from Peking University and a Ph.D. in economics from the University of Chicago. She served as a member of the National Academies of Sciences, Engineering, and Medicine's Commission for Global Roadmap for Healthy Longevity; the Social, Behavioral, & Environmental Enablers for Healthy Longevity: A Workshop for the Global Roadmap for Healthy Longevity Initiative; and the Panel on Policy Research and Data Needs to Meet the Challenge of Aging in Asia.